T0312842

PRAISE F
SIMPLY SPIRIT FILLED

"Whether you're curious about who the Holy Spirit is, just encountered Him for the first time, or are completely burned out on the subject, this book balances the more charismatic experiences of God with a thoughtful and thorough theology lesson, delivered from an honest and often humorous firsthand perspective. The Holy Spirit is the very manifestation of God in His people and this book will help the church encounter Him in a powerful new way."

—SAMUEL RODRIGUEZ, PRESIDENT OF THE NATIONAL
HISPANIC CHRISTIAN LEADERSHIP CONFERENCE;
TV HOST OF TBN's THE LAMB'S AGENDA

"Andrew Gabriel encourages readers to be discerning but also open to experiencing the Spirit. Gabriel writes with pastoral insight and personal experience while drawing on the depths of scholarship in a way that all Christians can benefit. I am pleased to recommend Simply Spirit-Filled to you."

—GEORGE O. WOOD, CHAIRMAN OF THE
WORLD ASSEMBLIES OF GOD FELLOWSHIP

"Andrew has a wonderful way of blending theology and application so that each reader will be more aware of the Holy Spirit in both the scriptures and daily living."

—SARAH BOWLING, COHOST OF THE TV
SHOW TODAY WITH MARILYN AND SARAH

"This marvelous book will help you make sense of how God by his Spirit works in our lives. Gabriel allows us to follow his life experience and walk with him as he touches base with the biblical text and helps us understand how the experiences of a Spirit encounter is what God has for us all. I'm so grateful for this book. It will bring clarity to confusion, and it will explain the legitimate life in the Spirit to those afraid of excess."

—BRIAN C. STILLER, GLOBAL AMBASSADOR,
THE WORLD EVANGELICAL ALLIANCE

"Andrew Gabriel presents a 'skeptic/junkie' dialectic concerning the presence and work of the Holy Spirit in the life of the twenty-first-century believer in a novel manner. He describes the synthesis of the polarities in terms of a refreshing spiritual maturity that engages the Spirit without abusing Him."

—JIM CANTELON, TV HOST OF *JIM CANTELON TODAY*

"I appreciate Dr. Andrew Gabriel as a colleague who shares his insight and perspectives with wisdom, honesty, and a good sense of humor. In *Simply Spirit-Filled* Andrew brings wholeness, passion, and wisdom to a reader's understanding of life in the Spirit. It is enhanced by being couched within the crucible of his own journey. There is a practicality and openness regarding the Spirit's person and work that will contribute to both the experienced believer and to those who are seeking to understand life in the Spirit."

—DAVID WELLS, GENERAL SUPERINTENDENT OF
THE PENTECOSTAL ASSEMBLIES OF CANADA

"We have long needed a biblically rooted, pastorally sensitive, and theologically well-informed evaluation of 'experiences of the Holy Spirit' and Andrew Gabriel has provided precisely that. This book is clearly and concisely written and should prove immensely helpful to all believers, even those who remain unpersuaded by his arguments. I highly recommend it."

—SAM STORMS, LEAD PASTOR FOR PREACHING AND
VISION AT BRIDGEWAY CHURCH, OKLAHOMA CITY, OK

"In his new book *Simply Spirit-Filled*, Andrew Gabriel writes with focus and scriptural balance. This book will be an appreciated resource to the Pentecostal church."

—TIM HILL, GENERAL OVERSEER,
CHURCH OF GOD, CLEVELAND, TN

"Andrew Gabriel writes with depth and yet simplicity, here clearing away the brush that plagues the contemporary pentecostal-charismatic movement. All pentecostal and charismatic believers should read this book for a more informed yet relevantly and biblically vibrant Spirit-empowered life. All their friends who have been burned by high-voltage charismatic experience or hurt by pentecostal churches should read this book to see how the Holy Spirit can revitalize their spirits. All pastors across this movement in all its diversity should read this book so they can lead their congregations more effectively into the twenty-first century."

—AMOS YONG, DIRECTOR OF THE CENTER FOR
MISSIOLOGICAL RESEARCH AND PROFESSOR OF THEOLOGY
AND MISSION, FULLER THEOLOGICAL SEMINARY

SIMPLY SPIRIT-FILLED

EXPERIENCING GOD IN THE
PRESENCE AND POWER
OF THE HOLY SPIRIT

SIMPLY SPIRIT-FILLED

ANDREW K. GABRIEL, PHD

EMANATE
BOOKS

© 2019 Andrew K. Gabriel

All rights reserved. No portion of this book may be reproduced, stored in a retrieval system, or transmitted in any form or by any means—electronic, mechanical, photocopy, recording, scanning, or other—except for brief quotations in critical reviews or articles, without the prior written permission of the publisher.

Published in Nashville, Tennessee, by Emanate Books, an imprint of Thomas Nelson. Emanate Books and Thomas Nelson are registered trademarks of HarperCollins Christian Publishing, Inc.

Thomas Nelson titles may be purchased in bulk for educational, business, fund-raising, or sales promotional use. For information, please e-mail SpecialMarkets@ThomasNelson .com.

Unless otherwise noted, Scripture quotations are taken from the Holy Bible, New International Version®, NIV®. Copyright © 1973, 1978, 1984, 2011 by Biblica, Inc.® Used by permission of Zondervan. All rights reserved worldwide. www.Zondervan.com. The "NIV" and "New International Version" are trademarks registered in the United States Patent and Trademark Office by Biblica, Inc.®

Scripture quotations marked ESV are from the ESV® Bible (The Holy Bible, English Standard Version®). Copyright © 2001 by Crossway, a publishing ministry of Good News Publishers. Used by permission. All rights reserved.

Scripture quotations marked NASB are from New American Standard Bible®. Copyright © 1960, 1962, 1963, 1968, 1971, 1972, 1973, 1975, 1977, 1995 by The Lockman Foundation. Used by permission. (www.Lockman.org)

Scripture quotations marked NLT are from the Holy Bible, New Living Translation. © 1996, 2004, 2007, 2013, 2015 by Tyndale House Foundation. Used by permission of Tyndale House Publishers, Inc., Carol Stream, Illinois 60188. All rights reserved.

Scripture quotations marked NRSV are from New Revised Standard Version Bible. Copyright © 1989 National Council of the Churches of Christ in the United States of America. Used by permission. All rights reserved.

All emphasis in Scripture quotations has been added by the author.

Any Internet addresses, phone numbers, or company or product information printed in this book are offered as a resource and are not intended in any way to be or to imply an endorsement by Thomas Nelson, nor does Thomas Nelson vouch for the existence, content, or services of these sites, phone numbers, companies, or products beyond the life of this book.

ISBN 978-0-7852-2362-7 (eBook)
ISBN 978-0-7852-2361-0 (TP)

Library of Congress Control Number: 2018962472

CONTENTS

CONTENTS

To Adelyn, Mylah, and Rayelle:

May you seek to live each day filled with the Spirit.

CHAPTER 1

CONFESSIONS OF A RECOVERING SPIRIT-EXPERIENCE JUNKIE

W hen I was eight, my family packed our boxes again and drove eighty miles to live near the Air Force Base in Greenwood, a town with just enough farming and military families to support a small mall with a Walmart. We were always moving because of my father's work, and so I grew up singing and praying in a number of different Baptist, Salvation Army, and primarily Pentecostal churches. Each church was unique in how they worshipped God, and each had distinct perspectives regarding what it meant to experience the Holy Spirit. The first time I remember having a real experience of the Holy Spirit was in Greenwood, in a modest Pentecostal church with brick and white siding and gravel in the parking lot. This is where the Spirit called me to put my faith in God.

I may have experienced the Holy Spirit in a service at another church a couple of years earlier, when I was six or seven years old, but I question whether this was the case. I remember shuffling to the front of the sanctuary and up the stairs onto the stage where the pastor guided a number of nervous children to stand side by side in a line. He prayed for us, and we fell over. Of course, we knew we were supposed to fall because the pastor had asked our parents to stand behind us to catch us. I don't recall much from this experience other than that I lay on the floor for a while and, the next day, when I played in my backyard with my neighbor, we stood one in front of the other on the grass and took turns catching each other as we fell backward. The fact that I remember anything about this experience, even though I was still quite young, makes me think I might have had an authentic encounter with God during the church service. At the same time, I wonder if I found myself on the floor solely as a result of charismatic manipulation.

After living in Greenwood, my faith in God meant little to me until my teenage years. Then, becoming serious about my faith meant regularly praying and reading my Bible, but also that I wanted to have lots of experiences of God. I'll describe some of these experiences in the coming chapters. Looking back, I'm not sure that all of them were legitimate. To some extent I just copied what other "Spirit-filled" people were doing. I watched people shake, so I shook. I heard people pray in tongues, and eventually I did as well. Following altar calls, during what we called the after service, that is, after the pastor preached and gave an invitation for people to gather at the front of the sanctuary and pray around the altar, I saw people laugh and dance, so I, too, laughed and danced. And I witnessed people stumble around as they claimed to be drunk in the Spirit, and sometimes I copied their stumbling.

I did all this because I yearned to know God or, probably more, to experience God. And experiencing God was like getting a spiritual high—a feeling of elation and peace. Even though I would diligently sit in my pew during a church service and concentrate on the sermon, I would eagerly await the after service. When it finally came, I would race to the altar because that was the place I sensed the presence of God the strongest. Furthermore, every summer you could find me at church camp, where it seemed the exciting spiritual stuff happened and I could experience the Spirit even more! After all, at camp there were altar calls every night of the week. While I have no doubt that the Spirit was forming me in positive ways during my teenage years, you might say that I became a bit of a Spirit-experience junkie.

The Junkie Turns Skeptic

Somewhere during my four years of college, I lost a sense of enchantment regarding the Spirit. I learned to be more discerning, or, you might say, to think more critically. For the most part this was a good thing, and I'm grateful for my time at college. I certainly learned how to understand the Bible there, and I even had the privilege of studying for a year in Africa, where I worshipped amid the explosion of global Christianity, much of which is Pentecostal or Charismatic in nature. But gradually, by my senior year of college, I started to become skeptical regarding my past experiences of the Spirit. It wasn't because of anything specific my professors taught me, but their encouragement to think about my faith did cause me to question the extent to which I was simply following the spiritual crowd.

That growing skepticism was also in part an overreaction to the revivals taking place during those years in Florida and Toronto. Some of my friends who had traveled there told me some Christians there were barking like dogs as some sort of spiritual experience, while others lay on the floor groaning as though they were giving birth to a child. I balked at these behaviors, which just seemed weird to me, and I hesitated to engage in any spiritual experiences that were associated with those revivals. This included anything happening there that resembled my previous experiences, sometimes even something as simple as raising my hands in worship.

After I graduated from college I got married, and we moved to a midsized city on the shore of one of the Great Lakes. There, in seminary, my skepticism reached its peak. As I continued to study, I questioned even more than just experiences of the Spirit. While I had caring and thoughtful pastors, for a while I had a hard time listening to their sermons because I could always find something to disagree with. And I wasn't so quick to respond to altar calls.

From Skepticism to Recovery

It wasn't as if all my studying caused me to lose my faith in God, though. In fact, it saved me. Reading theology was like reading devotional literature, and it deepened both my prayer life and my worship, helping me to recover from my skepticism. Over time I learned to relax more in church, to have a greater appreciation for the sermons I listened to, and to be less cynical about the experiences of the Spirit the people around me were claiming to have.

During these years of study, Krista (my wife), our girls, and I attended a large, multi-staffed church where the presence of the Spirit was evident in many ways. While I don't doubt that some things that happened at the church were more human-inspired than Spirit-inspired, both the pastors and the members of the congregation were outstanding examples of what it means to live a Spirit-filled life—they were passionate in their worship of God, they engaged in all the gifts of the Spirit on a regular basis, they prayed for and cared for one another, and they served communities around them and around the globe. During my time at that church, I slowly became more open to experiencing the Spirit in dramatic ways again. To some extent, my sense of enchantment regarding the Spirit returned, though now it coexisted with thoughtful discernment.

After completing my PhD, I moved to serve in the Midwest. Churches here on the prairies are not as vibrant as many churches where I have worshipped in the past. Yet, even though people here clap less during worship and aren't likely to shout "Amen!" when the preacher says something they like, I have still found the Spirit at work, though perhaps more quietly than I was used to. Thankfully, by now I have recovered from both my time as a Spirit-experience junkie and my time as a skeptic. As a result, I can appreciate that the Spirit works in and through believers in a variety of ways, some of which are less visible than others.

My Heart

I've met many people with stories similar to mine—people who were once open to having intense experiences of the Spirit, experiences that might affect their emotions and even their bodies, but who were turned off by some seemingly strange people they witnessed in a worship service or even some strange experiences they may have had themselves. Some have watched people try to manipulate others under the guise of the spiritual gifts. Others have seen people fake an experience of the Spirit. Some have been discouraged by seeing too many pastors or evangelists, who were supposedly anointed by the Spirit, betray others' trust with terrible moral failures. Such experiences could make anyone want to stay away from anything that has to do with the Holy Spirit.

I've met many other people who have never been open

to experiencing the Holy Spirit in any perceptible manner. Usually they are from churches where the Spirit is never discussed, or, if the Spirit is mentioned, it is usually in a negative way. They are warned, "Be careful of people who talk too much about the Holy Spirit," as though the Spirit were like poison or a hot stove. "Don't get too close! Don't touch!"

The Holy Spirit is not hazardous. Jesus was anointed by the Spirit, and we all love Jesus (Acts 10:38). And if you are a Christian, you can't escape the Holy Spirit anyway, because the Spirit dwells within you, making you "a temple of the Holy Spirit" (1 Corinthians 6:19 NASB). If it wasn't for the Holy Spirit living in us, God might seem only far off in heaven or in the distant past doing miracles in Galilee. Thankfully, "this is how we know that [God] lives in us: We know it by the Spirit he gave us" (1 John 3:24).

The Holy Spirit is like the wind. In fact, the Hebrew and Greek words for *Spirit* (the languages the Bible was originally written in) both mean "wind." And like the wind, the Spirit is mysterious. It is free and unpredictable and shapes its surroundings (John 3:8). Sometimes the wind gusts powerfully like a hurricane, whereas at other times it blows gently and we are not conscious of its stirring. Some Christians only look for the Spirit in the storm—in the spectacular and dramatic. By contrast, others assume the Spirit is only ever a calm breeze. We should not deny that the wind of the Spirit blows both powerfully and gently.

My hope for the skeptic is that you will be open to experiencing the Holy Spirit, who is the touch of God, as more than just idly dwelling within you, and that you would sense the Spirit like "a spring of water welling up" within (John 4:14). My hope for the Spirit-experience junkie is that you will be discerning and realize that we experience the Spirit for more than just selfish reasons, like to enjoy a psychedelic buzz during worship. My hope for everyone is that you would "not quench the Spirit . . . but test everything; hold fast to what is good" (1 Thessalonians 5:19, 21 NRSV). Open, but not gullible. Discerning, but not cynical. Engaging, but not fanatical. My hope is that you would be simply Spirit-filled.

Father, for those of us who have been skeptical or feared the Holy Spirit, please open our hearts to the authentic work of the Spirit. For those of us who have not followed your direction to test everything, help us be more discerning. Blow like the wind, Holy Spirit, in our lives.

Questions for Reflection or Discussion

1. Do you think you have leaned more toward being a Spirit-experience junkie or toward being a skeptic of experiences of the Spirit?
2. What are some ways you have experienced the Holy Spirit?

3. What is the most intense experience of the Spirit you have had?
4. Do you equally value the ways the Spirit blows like a strong wind and like a calm breeze?
5. What does it mean to be open to having authentic experiences of the Spirit?

CHAPTER 2

SHAKE AND BAKE

Slain in the Spirit and Other Manifestations

The steel concave walls made the sanctuary, or tabernacle, as we called it, look more like a steel barn than a church. About a dozen campers remained in the evening worship service, praying and singing the slow worship choruses as the band played their guitars and keyboard onstage. Below the stage, I lay flat on my back on the cold concrete floor. I opened my eyes and saw the green plastic underside of a chair. Later my roommate would tell me that when I fell back my head smacked the chair and then cracked on the floor. Yet I had no sense of this or any pain as I lay there, and there would be no negative after-effects.

My experience that night was what many people call being "slain in the Spirit." Some people also refer to this as "falling under the power" of God or "resting in the Spirit." The idea is that, while people are worshipping, the Holy Spirit might "slay" them by making them fall over as if dead. Of course, if you have ever been in a church service where you have seen this happen, you will know as well as I do that many people who fall over are not knocked over by the Holy Spirit; they are pushed over by a preacher.

Slain in the Spirit

But no one pushed me over when I fell under that chair at church camp. On previous occasions I had been prayed for and had people catch me when I fell over. But this time was different. I wanted to know if the experience of being slain in the Spirit was legitimate. Perhaps I was a bit naive; I was still in my teens. If I had resolved to test the experience of being slain in the Spirit later in life, I'm sure I would have gone about it differently. But that night, as I stood there worshipping with my hands raised, I began to feel myself sway like a tree that was being cut down. This is what usually happened before I was slain in the Spirit. I suspect this was more my own doing than that of the Holy Spirit. After all, I eagerly desired to have "more of God," as the preachers put it, and this especially included feeling or sensing God more—what some people describe as mystical experiences of God. But as I swayed, I knew that this time there was no hand behind my back to catch me. The time had come for the test.

So I let myself fall. Did I mention that the floor was concrete? The camp had apparently stopped believing in having sawdust on the floor at the altar, as some earlier generations did. Still, I didn't feel my head hitting the floor or the chair. I have heard stories of other people falling down while worshipping and without experiencing pain as well.

Shaking and Baking

Being slain in the Spirit is only one of the controversial so-called manifestations of the Spirit. Another one would be shaking. I myself have shaken to some extent. Usually it was just one arm or one leg at a time. I have also seen some people shake quite violently, so much that you might wonder if they were demon possessed or having a seizure.

I jokingly describe the trembling as the shake and the lying there "under the power" as the bake. I myself have experienced both. During the numerous times I have lain on the floor "baking," I have remained conscious of myself and those worshipping around me. Sometimes I have also prayed, sometimes I have prayed in tongues, and sometimes I have sung, but I think the majority of the time I just lay there relaxing and soaking in the presence of God. And while I have absolutely no doubt that I encountered God in those moments, I do want to question whether the shaking and falling were actually from God.

Are the Experiences Caused by the Spirit?

I really did meet with God the night I fell and cracked my head on the concrete floor, but maybe it was not the Holy Spirit who made me fall down. Maybe I fell down because I wanted to. But what about the fact that I didn't end up with a concussion or bump on my head after it hit the floor? Perhaps that was God being gracious to me in my naiveté. God knew my faith was sincere, even though I was possibly putting God to the test. Instead of healing me after the fact, maybe the Lord was gracious enough to keep me from injuring myself in the first place. This is certainly possible. But even if God miraculously saved me from injury, my falling does not require us to conclude that the Holy Spirit knocked me over.

And what about those experiences when I shook? My shaking does not require any supernatural explanation either. I had seen other people do it. I probably came to the conclusion that that was what a person was to expect when they experienced the Holy Spirit during a church service. So, again, I ask the question: what are we to make of all this trembling and falling?

The Loopy and Weird Test

One could immediately reject experiences of falling or shaking as just plain weird. I hear some people dismiss certain teachings or experiences simply because they sound loopy. The problem with this approach, however, is that we usually make such conclusions only when it concerns an experience we are not used to; yet, others may be very used to it. Nevertheless, many people have made similar conclusions regarding speaking in tongues. In fact, numerous times throughout Christian history, church leaders have accused people who spoke in tongues of being demon possessed. If the Pentecostal-Charismatic movement had not grown to the extent it has today, speaking in tongues would still seem weird—it remains so for some people—and many people would continue to dismiss the experience of speaking in tongues as a result. So I do not think it is wise to dismiss trembling or falling under the power of the Spirit just because it seems strange.

A First Look at Scripture

Unlike my own testing of God in my youth, a better way for us to test the idea of trembling or being slain in the Spirit is to consider the Scripture. This might seem like a dead end, perhaps a dead end that settles the question. After all, the phrases "slain in the Spirit" and "falling under the power" never occur in the Scripture. By contrast, references to "speaking in tongues" do appear a number of times. In spite of the missing phrases, however, some people do claim to find examples of people being slain in the Spirit in the Bible.

When I went looking, I found that one of the most common verses people refer to in support of being slain in the Spirit comes from the night Jesus was arrested. Some soldiers and officials approached Jesus to arrest him. When they said they were looking for Jesus, Jesus affirmed, "I am he," and then the soldiers "drew back and fell to the ground" (John 18:6). It should be obvious from the context of this verse that it does not provide biblical support for the experience of being slain in the Spirit. These were soldiers who came to arrest Jesus. And their experience of falling had no immediate positive effect on them, because it seems they weren't converted, and they did indeed arrest Jesus. This passage might seem helpful for supporting the idea of being slain in the Spirit if we only focus on the fact that people "fell to the ground." But once we realize these people were not at all seeking the presence of God and that they were not even Christians, it is clear that this verse provides weak support for being slain in the Spirit.

We must say the same thing regarding the soldiers who guarded Jesus' tomb. They encountered the angel of the Lord and "were so afraid of him that they shook and became like dead men" (Matthew 28:4). This story has next to no resemblance to contemporary stories of people shaking or being slain in the Spirit in the context of a worship service, except for the fact that in both instances people shook and fell to the ground.

Falling Before the Lord

Nevertheless, many other scriptures speak of people falling before the Lord. On the one hand, in some cases a person chooses to fall over as a reverent response in worship to God, rather than being knocked over by God. For example, "Joshua fell on his face to the earth" before the Lord. We know that Joshua fell by his own initiative, for this verse also clarifies that Joshua "bowed low" (Joshua 5:14 NASB; Numbers 22:31).

On the other hand, a number of biblical texts do not make it clear if the person falls before the Lord intentionally or not. For example, in Genesis 17:3 we are only told that "Abram fell on his face, and God talked with him" (NASB). Similarly, in Judges 13:20 we read, "As the flame blazed up from the altar toward heaven, the angel of the LORD ascended in the flame. Seeing this, Manoah and his wife fell with their faces to the ground." While these verses allow for the possibility that these people fell involuntarily and were, therefore, slain in the Spirit, nothing explicit in the context of these verses leads me to think this is what happened. Therefore, I came to the conclusion that the biblical authors had no intention of teaching about the experience of being slain in the Spirit, if it is in the Bible at all.

Furthermore, most texts in Scripture that describe people as falling before God are describing experiences quite different from the ones many Christians today call being slain in the Spirit. For example, in many of the verses I mentioned above, the individual who falls before the Lord falls forward. By contrast, most who claim to have been slain in the Spirit fall backward. In some biblical texts where people fall forward before God, it is clear that they do not continue to lay there basking in the presence of God, as people who are slain in the Spirit today generally do. In fact, sometimes those who fall down before God are immediately told to "arise." This is what happened at the transfiguration of Jesus. Peter, James, and John hiked up a mountain with Jesus. Jesus was then "transfigured before them; and His face shone like the sun, and His garments became as white as light" (Matthew 17:2 NASB). As a result, Peter, James, and John "fell face down to the ground and were terrified" (v. 6 NASB). Jesus responded to their falling by saying, "Get up, and do not be afraid" (v. 7 NASB). So Peter, James, and John didn't keep lying there.

This is quite different from how many people describe their experiences of having been slain in the Spirit. Furthermore, the typical setting where people claim to be slain in the Spirit clearly does not occur in Scripture. Nowhere in the Bible can you find a preacher giving an altar call and lining up people with catchers ready to catch those for whom the preacher prays. Also, no one is ever touched or prayed for when they fall in the Scripture.

A New Experience?

Since my first searching of the Scripture suggested that being slain in the Spirit and shaking was not a biblical idea,

I eventually came to the conclusion that being slain in the Spirit was a new event in Christianity. By new, I mean an idea people made up in the last few decades and that had no basis in the Scripture. As a result, I began to associate being slain in the Spirit with the excesses of some revivalistic worship that make many people balk. As I studied church history, however, it became apparent that I was mistaken to only associate being slain in the Spirit with contemporary Charismatic movements or fringe groups.

Experiences of people falling under the power of God were common in the early days of the Pentecostal-Charismatic movement. The Azusa Street Revival was one of the most important events at the beginning of this movement. The revival took place in Los Angeles, California, from 1906 to 1909. There it was common for people to fall under the power of God during worship meetings. In the first edition of *The Apostolic Faith* newspaper, published from the Azusa Street Revival, one attendee testified, "So many are seeking, and some are slain under the power of God. . . . In the meetings, it is noticeable that while some in the rear are opposing and arguing, others are at the altar falling down under the power of God and feasting on the good things of God."[1] The first edition of *The Pentecostal Testimony*, a small newspaper published by the Pentecostal Assemblies of Canada, contained a similar report from Alberta: "In our Sunday morning meetings the power has been falling like rain. . . . Under the power of the Holy Ghost some fall prostrate, others dance, some sing, march around the Hall, shout the praises of Jesus, etc."[2]

Early Evangelicalism

It would be easy for people to make another mistake and conclude that being slain in the Spirit has only happened in the last hundred years during the contemporary Pentecostal-Charismatic movement. In fact, I have found a long history of such experiences. Let me take you further back in history to early evangelicalism. Historians agree that the evangelical movement began in the 1700s during the revival movements associated with people like Jonathan Edwards and John Wesley.

Jonathan Edwards (1703–1758) was a Calvinist who lived in New England. Calvinism is a major branch of Protestantism that follows the theological tradition and Christian practice of John Calvin and other Reformation theologians. While many remember Edwards for his famous sermon, "Sinners in the Hands of an Angry God," he was also one of America's greatest theologians and a key leader in the Great Awakening revival (1720–1740s). Regarding this time, Edwards wrote, "It was a very frequent thing to see a house full of outcries, faintings, convulsions, and such like, both with distress, and also with admiration and joy."[3]

Edwards believed that at least some of these fainting experiences and convulsions resulted from authentic encounters with God.

John Wesley (1703–1791) hailed from across the Atlantic Ocean in England. Although he is best known as the founder of the Methodist movement, which eventually led to Methodist denominations, he lived and died as an Anglican—the word used to describe the people, institutions, and churches, as well as the liturgical traditions and theological concepts developed by the Church of England. Like Edwards, Wesley was a theologian, though not a Calvinist, and a revivalist.

Wesley recounted numerous incidents when people fell or shook at meetings where he was preaching, especially "sinners" who were converted after such experiences. Wesley described people falling as one of the "outward signs that so often accompanied the inward work of God."[4] He reported that some of his critics claimed people fell on the ground only from "*natural* effects" in the sense that they "fainted away only because of the heat and closeness of the rooms."[5] Other critics suggested that when people fell it was all fake because the falling only happened in private meetings.

In response to such claims, Wesley wrote in his journal that on May 21, 1739, God "began to make bare his arm, not in a close room, neither in private, but in the open air, and before more than two thousand witnesses. One, and another, and another was struck to the earth; exceedingly trembling at the presence of His power."[6]

As evangelicalism moved into the next century, people occasionally experienced the same signs of the work of the Spirit that previous evangelicals had experienced. Falling and trembling were common experiences during the Second Great Awakening (1800–1840s). At this time, Presbyterians, Baptists, Methodists, and others started holding camp meetings. Concerning a camp meeting held in Georgia in the early 1800s, one person reported,

> They swooned away and lay for hours in the straw prepared for those "smitten of the Lord," or they started suddenly to flee away and fell prostrate as if shot down by a sniper, or they took suddenly to jerking with apparently every muscle in their body until it seemed they would be torn to pieces or converted into marble, or they shouted and talked in unknown tongues.[7]

The testimonies of Edwards, Wesley, and other early evangelicals made it clear to me that contemporary experiences of trembling in the presence of God or being slain in the Spirit are not new to the evangelical movement. While they were not always common, they did not begin with the dawn of the contemporary Pentecostal-Charismatic movement.

Reassessing Scripture

The fact that experiences of being slain in the Spirit and trembling are not new in Christian history and the fact that key leaders in early evangelicalism sometimes accepted them as authentic experiences of God does not prove that such experiences are legitimate. Nevertheless, these historical observations caused me to pause and reassess these experiences in light of Scripture. In the Bible, I found that although people who encountered God usually had control of themselves, people sometimes lost control or had involuntary responses to God's presence. For example, after Paul met Jesus on the road to Damascus, God continued to keep his attention by making him blind for three days (Acts 9:9). This was certainly not something Paul voluntarily made happen to himself. Trances also happened involuntarily. Peter "fell into a trance" and then had a vision from God (Acts 10:10). Likewise, the apostle Paul "fell into a trance" one day while praying in the temple (Acts 22:17).

And They Trembled

I also found some testimonies in the Bible of people trembling before the Lord. For example, one psalmist wrote, "My flesh trembles in fear of you" (Psalm 119:120). Beyond this, when the presence of the Lord descended on Mount Sinai, "the whole mountain trembled violently" (Exodus 19:18). If God's presence can make a mountain tremble, it makes good sense for us to think that a person might respond to God's presence with trembling.

Humans are more than just minds and thoughts, so it is natural that God would not only renew our minds (Romans 12:2), but that some intense encounters would also affect our emotions and our bodies.[8] I am not suggesting that God shakes people to *make* them tremble or fall, although God could. Instead, it might be that people shake or tremble as a reaction to the presence of God, just as some people weep in God's presence. Similarly, it might be helpful to think of being slain in the Spirit as a human reaction to the presence of God working in or around a person. In other words, sometimes God's presence or work in a person could be so overwhelming that a person might tremble or fall— not because God is slaying them and making them fall, not because God is pushing them over, but because *they just can't stand* in the presence of God any longer.

We do find a few examples in Scripture of God's presence affecting people's ability to stand. After Solomon built the first temple to the Lord, the temple "was filled with a cloud." What was the result? "The priests could not stand to minister because of the cloud, for the glory of the LORD filled the house of the LORD" (2 Chronicles 5:13–14; 1 Kings 8:10–11 ESV). Also, as in the stories of "sinners" who fell prostrate before being converted in the revival meetings of early evangelicalism, Saul, later called Paul, was traveling to Damascus to persecute Christians and, after experiencing a bright light, "he fell to the ground" (Acts 9:4). Stories like these about Paul and the priests in the temple make me wonder if some of the stories I discussed earlier in the chapter might have been similar experiences, even if they are not as explicit and do not clearly say why the person fell or what caused the person to fall. For example, could it be that "Abram fell on his face" involuntarily before God talked to him (Genesis 17:3 ESV)? This could be a parallel to where Peter and Paul fell into a trance before God spoke to them in visions. It is also possible that when John saw the resurrected Jesus, John "fell at his feet as though dead" involuntarily (Revelation 1:17). As I noted, sometimes the Bible doesn't say whether the person "fell down" before the Lord on purpose or involuntarily. We don't always know. We do know, however, that in at least some cases, people could not stand as a result of God's presence.

Illegitimate Manifestations

All I found in my study of history and the Bible did not, however, cause me to accept that every time a person falls or shakes in a church service they are doing so because of the presence of God. I have come to think that *sometimes* this is the case—but probably not that often.

Many leaders of historical revivals have been well aware that there were both legitimate and illegitimate manifestations of the Spirit happening in the meetings they led. William Durham was one of them. Durham led a revival in Chicago in the early 1900s that eventually over-shadowed the revival at Azusa Street. Durham complained of "fanatics" who would claim that every strange physical manifestation was from God. On the opposite side were fanatics who charged that everything out of the ordinary was from the Devil or demons. Even though Durham did believe that some manifestations were caused by Satan, he did not regard the presence of the fanatics as a reason to reject completely all that happened at revival meetings. Instead, he deemed their presence a sign of spiritual vitality. Expressing this, Durham wrote,

> Every great revival attracts not only honest seekers and well-balanced people, but cranks and fanatics. I never saw the exception. Every revivalist of any note has had his troubles with them, and we have had our full share. There is a host of them and they all desire to air their theories or ride their hobbies; but they are no proof that God is not working, but rather prove that He is working.

Like Durham, we don't have to completely reject or completely accept every strange experience as a manifestation of the presence of God, including falling or shaking. Furthermore, thinking these experiences can come only from God or the Devil is also too limiting. I agree with Durham's assessment that, in addition, "in many genuine experiences the flesh is allowed to get in some little measure."[9]

Peer Pressure

Besides God or the Devil, there are many other reasons a person might shake or fall. For example, a person might shake because that is what they saw someone else do and they, therefore, came to the conclusion that if you are Spirit-filled or experiencing the presence of God, you are supposed to shake. I'm convinced this happened to me.

Alternatively, I'm sure that many people have fallen down in a church service due to peer pressure. Sometimes the peer pressure is subtle—they may have just watched the preacher pray for five people who fell down, and now the preacher is going to pray for them. There is now pressure for them to fall down too. At other times the peer pressure is more evident. I remember one service where the preacher called all the young people to the altar, lined them up, and told them that they were going to fall under the power of God. The pastor proceeded to wave his jacket across the crowd of youth yelling, "Fresh wind!" They fell down, of course. After all, it would have been embarrassing to have been the only person left standing.

Sometimes peer pressure is even literal pressure. One day my wife was visiting another church, and while she was worshipping God in response to the altar call, she noticed that the preacher was walking around and praying for those who had gathered at the altar. He placed his hand on some people's foreheads and pushed them backward until they fell down. Rather than waiting to see how persistent he would be in his methods, Krista knelt down on the floor so she could escape his ministry, and she continued to worship God.

Other practices found at some revival meetings could be considered forms of peer pressure, even if they are more innocent. For example, some pastors ensure that when they pray for others there are "catchers" behind the people they are praying for. But there are no catchers in the Bible. Even though these pastors mean well by ensuring those who fall down don't hurt themselves, I have a feeling these catchers are often just as important for the pastor praying, because the catchers indicate to the people being prayed for that they should get ready to fall down . . . but not until the pastor prays for them. Now is a good time to remind ourselves that there are no stories in Scripture where somebody falls under the power of God as someone else is praying for them.

Where Is the Fruit?

Despite certain abuses, I do still recognize that some people will have authentic experiences of God in which their bodies will respond by shaking or falling. The fruit or outcome of such experiences sometimes testifies to their authenticity. During the Great Awakenings, sinners' experience of falling in services would often lead them to make a decision to follow Jesus Christ. This is a desirable outcome. Positive fruit can also be found among some Christians who have experienced being slain in the Spirit or shaking. One pastor interviewed people about their experiences of being slain in the Spirit, and they described their experiences in this way:

> A warm glow, a sweetness, a certain peace. One person said it was "heavenly peace." Others describe it as "a real faith builder," or "It really established my confidence." "It took away my doubts" is another expression that is used to explain its effect. . . . One person said she received a definite answer to prayer that has since affected her whole life. Another spoke of seeing a vision of the Lord. Still another talked of "everything around becoming insignificant," and another of sensing great love from the Father.[10]

Sometimes Christians who are averse to falling in the presence of God find themselves swept off their feet and experiencing the Spirit in a way that brings positive results. One non-charismatic Baptist pastor recalled visiting a service at a charismatic church and wrote,

> As I stood to receive prayer, I was determined not to fall down as some did, wanting to worship Jesus and invite his presence in my own way. But then my legs completely melted, and I fell backwards to the carpet for several minutes. My mind was still alert, wondering, until convulsions started in my stomach, and I began heaving sobs from the pit of my being. A sense of peace followed my crying in which I knew that I was deeply known, forgiven, and loved in the presence of God. He also used this time to give me insight into my ongoing sin patterns, reassurance that deep emotional wounds were being healed, and reaffirmation of my direction for ministry.[11]

Similar to the above testimonies, a friend of mine has fallen under the power of God three times in her life. She believes that each time this occurred God was preparing her to face a significant personal challenge. At one point she was feeling anxious due to a major career change she was anticipating. On top of this, her house was not selling and she was moving to an area where the cost of real estate was higher, and some people were questioning the wisdom of her decision to move. Then, one day at the end of a church service, she sensed God's presence and fell down. When she eventually returned to her feet, she felt affirmed in God's love, with her faith strengthened, and with a renewed sense of peace about her career change.

Additional Cautions

Although the previous stories show that some people have had positive experiences after they have trembled or fallen under the power of God, I would never want to suggest that every Christian should seek or expect to have these experiences. If you are ever disappointed that God didn't knock you over or that you didn't sense God's presence to such an extent that you shook, there may be a problem in your heart—it might indicate that you are seeking an experience of God rather than seeking an intimate relationship with God. Don't feel condemned if you have ever felt this way, though. I know I have had this feeling myself.

I think of Moses and his encounter with God at the burning bush (Exodus 3), and I am reminded that many people in the Bible had intimate and intense encounters with God without losing control of themselves in any way—they didn't have to shake or fall. Therefore, we should not make the dangerous conclusion that out-of-the-ordinary experiences with God are indicators of our spiritual vitality (more on this in a later chapter). Remember, falling or shaking was not a normal experience for people in the Bible. These experiences are *unusual* precisely because they are *out of the ordinary*. So we should not expect them to happen ordinarily or try to manufacture them. Moreover, people who have never experienced shaking or falling should not feel guilty. If God really wanted all Christians to have and expect these experiences, I'm sure God would have made this clearer in the Bible.

Transformed in God's Presence

Allow me to bring you back to my story from the beginning of this chapter. In light of all that I have said here, how would I now evaluate my experience that evening at church camp? I still remain unconvinced that I have ever fallen down because the Holy Spirit knocked me over. I am fully aware that I was not just *open* to being slain in the Spirit, but rather, I *wanted* to fall down at that point in my life. Regardless, one thing I know for sure is that I met with God in those moments and those encounters had a vital role in shaping me into who I am today. During those moments the holiness and majesty of God became real to me, God spoke to me, and my faith and commitment to God increased. In fact, if I had not experienced God in those ways, I don't know where I would be today.

Aside from my own experiences, I have concluded that at many times in history, people have shaken or fallen down simply because they could no longer stand in the presence of God. This is not quite the same thing as being "slain," which seems to imply that a person is knocked over by God, but it is consistent with the idea of "falling under the power" of God. At the same time, however, I suspect that many, and perhaps even most, people who claim to have been slain in the Spirit experienced this of their own volition, or because someone pushed them over, or because they believed that was what they were supposed to do. Nevertheless, I do not doubt that in the midst of these experiences, even those people who have caused themselves, out of immaturity, to shake or fall have still experienced the power and presence of God in life-altering ways.

Remember, God is gracious and continues to work despite our immaturity and weaknesses. On account of this, we need to be careful of discrediting other people's experiences of being slain in the Spirit. Like a musician who is jamming with friends can play the wrong note without being condemned for doing something terrible, in some cases Christians (this was my own experience) need to have permission to relax and occasionally hit the wrong note in order to authentically experience the Holy Spirit. When all is said and done, while we should not seek nor manufacture so-called manifestations of the Spirit, we should welcome legitimate, intense encounters with God's presence when they come. And if you should ever find yourself reacting to God with shaking or falling, continue to worship God and wait to see what God may want to speak to you in that moment.

Thank you, Lord, that we can experience the Holy Spirit in intense ways that remind us that you are with us. Forgive us if we have ever pretended to experience the Spirit or if we have tried to force experiences of the Spirit upon others. We acknowledge that we cannot control your presence, and we pray that you would continue to pour out your Spirit upon us.

Questions for Reflection or Discussion

1. What in Scripture suggests that, in some instances, a person might respond to the presence of God with trembling or by falling?
2. If you have ever shaken or fallen while worshipping God, what was this experience like for you?
3. How have you felt toward those who experienced the Spirit in ways such as shaking or falling when you weren't having a similar experience yourself?
4. How do you feel about those who seek to manufacture these experiences of the Spirit rather than allow them to occur as unordinary and uncommon experiences?
5. Why do you suppose the Spirit sometimes seems to overwhelm certain people?

CHAPTER 3

KNOCK, KNOCK. WHO'S THERE?

Hearing God Speak

G od told me to marry you."

No one ever said this to my wife or me, although I suppose it would have made things a little simpler if God had just told us to marry each other, but it is repeated as a running joke at many Christian colleges. The sad thing is that this joke has a basis in reality, because too many times God has supposedly told one person who to marry, but has neglected to tell the other person. And the other person is usually not too thrilled about the idea. Or worse, she has clearly heard God tell her *not* to marry the first person. Needless to say, in most instances the two people don't get married, at least not to each other. Perhaps God is confused. Or, more likely, one person has been trying to spiritualize their feelings for the other person.

Perhaps you can remember a time when someone claimed that God told them something, when in reality it seemed that person was trying to impose their will and desires on others. Situations like these can make us skeptical about the whole idea of hearing God speak.

My Own Skepticism

When I was in my early twenties, I came to the conclusion that God doesn't speak today. Or, if God does speak, it doesn't happen often. Like many young adults, I was wrestling with major life decisions, like what vocation I should pursue and where I should live after college. As a result, I investigated a number of books about finding God's will, and I even wrote a paper on that topic in my third year of college. One book I read, *Decision Making and the Will of God*, really got me thinking. It contained many valuable messages that I still nod my head in agreement with today.

I learned that the Lord doesn't necessarily want to whisper in my ear what I should do in every situation I face. Instead, God gives me wisdom to help *me* make decisions. This was accurate biblical teaching: "If any of you lacks wisdom, you should ask God, who gives generously to all without finding fault, and it will be given to you" (James 1:5). Nevertheless, the book also taught me that today God only communicates through the Scripture. The basic idea was that God has said in the Bible all that needs to be said, so the Lord doesn't need to speak today outside of the Bible. I remember sitting in a classroom one year after I read the book. Standing at the front, the professor smiled and asked, "Have any of you heard God speak to you?" Though I was embarrassed to admit it, I looked down at my desk and answered, "I used to think I had, but now I'm not so sure."

God Who Speaks

Eventually I had an aha moment. I was reading the Bible and realized that God spoke to the people who wrote the Bible. I reasoned that if God spoke directly to prophets and apostles, God can speak directly to anyone, and God could speak directly to me. After all, God's nature hasn't changed. It seems so obvious, but I had missed it, at least for a while.

Throughout the stories of the Bible, God regularly spoke to people. In the first pages of the Scripture, in the story of Adam and Eve, "God blessed them and said to them, 'Be fruitful and increase in number'" (Genesis 1:28). Later in Genesis 6:13–15, God said to Noah, "Make yourself an ark of cypress wood." Exodus 33:11 reports that "the LORD would speak to Moses face to face, as one speaks to a friend." When faced with oppression from the Midianites, God told Gideon, "Go in the strength you have and save Israel out of Midian's hand" (Judges 6:14). The prophet Jeremiah was hesitant to accept God's call, so God reassured him and said, "Do not say, 'I am too young.' . . . I am with you and will rescue you" (Jeremiah 1:7–8).

In the New Testament, no one locked up God's lips and threw away the key. At Jesus' baptism, the Father said, "This is my Son, whom I love; with him I am well pleased" (Matthew 3:17). And in numerous places in the New Testament, we are specifically told that the Holy Spirit was speaking to people. On one occasion, "the Spirit told Philip" to go near a chariot

(Acts 8:29). As a result, Philip ended up sharing the gospel with an Ethiopian who was then baptized. In another story, the church in Antioch was worshipping and fasting and "the Holy Spirit said, 'Set apart for me Barnabas and Saul [Paul] for the work to which I have called them'" (Acts 13:2). As a result, Barnabas and Paul set out on their first missionary journey. First Timothy 4:1 warns, "The Spirit clearly says that in later times some will abandon the faith." And, in numerous places the book of Revelation advises people to "hear what the Spirit says to the churches" (Revelation 2:7, 11, 17, 29; 3:6, 13, 22). The Spirit is not a vague force; the Spirit was and is still personal. And God speaks to us in the person of the Holy Spirit.

I am encouraged to find that God doesn't communicate only with the holiest or most spiritual people. The Lord spoke to Paul the apostle, despite the fact that before Paul became a Christian he had made plans to travel around killing believers (Acts 9:1–2). Moses actually did murder someone (Exodus 2:11–12). And after the Lord spoke to Gideon, Gideon lacked faith and told God why he shouldn't be the one to lead Israel (Judges 6:12–15). Even after God gave Gideon a miraculous sign to prove that God was speaking to him, Gideon continued to doubt and asked God to give him two more miraculous signs to convince him that God would do what God had said (Judges 6:36–40). While God might very well have given up in light of Gideon's lack of trust, God was gracious and still spoke to him. God has spoken to many imperfect people in the past, and today God continues to speak to imperfect people, like you and me.

God Speaks Through the Bible

When I say God speaks, I am referring to the different ways the Lord communicates with us. In the Bible, people actually did hear an audible voice from God sometimes, like when Jesus was baptized (Matthew 3:17). In most places in the Bible, however, when God speaks we are simply told that "God said," or that "the Lord responded," or that "the Spirit told," but we usually aren't told exactly *how* God spoke.

The most obvious way God speaks is by communicating through the Scripture. "All Scripture is God-breathed" (2 Timothy 3:16), so it is appropriate to think of the Bible as words God has spoken to us. Before we concern ourselves with hearing from God in other ways, we should always begin with listening well to what the Lord has already said to us in Scripture.

Beyond only reading the Bible to hear what God has said in the past, we should also realize that the Bible is a primary way God speaks to people in the present. God's Word is not some dusty artifact we discover hidden in the ancient history of the Bible. Rather, "the word of God is alive and active" and "it judges the thoughts and attitudes of the heart" (Hebrews 4:12).

On one occasion I was relaxing on my living room sofa reading through the parable of the lost sheep. In this story Jesus explains that if a shepherd loses a sheep, he will leave ninety-nine sheep to go and find the lost sheep and then rejoice with his friends when he finds the missing one (Luke 15:4–7).

God spoke to me through this passage of Scripture about how I needed to be more active in sharing the gospel with others. I wrote in my journal: "It says that the shepherd 'goes after' the lost sheep. He doesn't just wait to run into it. He is not passive, but purposeful. Lord, help me to be more purposeful." God has spoken to me through Scripture on many other occasions in similar ways.

Other Ways God Speaks

God speaks through the Bible, but the Lord's voice is not limited to the Bible. Jesus made this clear when he responded to a group of Jewish leaders who were harassing him and planning to kill him. While he recognized that these leaders would "study the Scriptures diligently" (John 5:39), at the same time he scolded them for their lack of relationship with the Father: "You have never heard his voice nor seen his form, nor does his word dwell in you" (vv. 37–38). Jesus' reprimand serves as a good reminder that our relationship is with God, not with the Bible.

In addition to speaking through Scripture, God also communicates with us through visions and dreams (Acts 2:17) as well as through other people by means of the gifts of the Spirit, such as prophecy. God could also speak to us through pictures or nature. My wife finds that God speaks to her especially through songs. There are many ways the Lord might speak to us.

Aside from the Bible, I find God usually speaks directly to my heart. You could describe it as a feeling, an impression, an intuition, or a thought in my conscience. Before Jesus was crucified, he sat down with his disciples and told them he would send the Holy Spirit to guide his followers (John 16:13). The apostle Paul explained that God "put his Spirit *in our hearts*" (2 Corinthians 1:22), so it makes sense that the Holy Spirit would guide us by speaking to our hearts. In scriptures about the Spirit speaking to people, this was most likely what was happening. Because "God sent the Spirit of his Son into our hearts" (Galatians 4:6), we, too—to use the words of Gordon Smith—have the "possibility of intimacy with Christ" and a "kind of immediacy to our relationship with God."[1]

Do I Need to Listen?

While I came to recognize that God does speak to people today, one thing that began to annoy me was when I heard people say that I have to *listen* more closely to hear God's voice. Preachers would often emphasize that God has "a still small voice." I thought, *Can't God speak loudly enough?* When I looked in the Bible, it seemed to me that people were not unsure of when the Lord spoke to them. For example, leading up to Paul's conversion to Christianity, he was walking on the road to Damascus, and he heard a voice plainly say, "Why do you persecute me?" (Acts 9:4). Couldn't God speak to me like that? Experiences like Paul's would remove any sense of uncertainty I might have about when God is speaking.

As I read my Bible, I was happy to find that God could and sometimes does speak loudly. David wrote,

> The voice of the LORD is over the waters;
> > the God of glory thunders,
> > the LORD thunders over the mighty waters.
> The voice of the LORD is powerful;
> > the voice of the LORD is majestic.
> The voice of the LORD breaks the cedars;
> > the LORD breaks in pieces the cedars of
> > Lebanon.
>
> **(PSALM 29:3–5)**

That is the kind of God I wanted to experience. A powerful God—a God who speaks out of fire on mountains (Deuteronomy 5:4) and whose voice scares the living daylights out of sinners.

Nevertheless, in spite of God's ability to speak loudly, the Lord can and does sometimes speak quietly. God told Elijah to go stand on a mountain so God could address him. There was a strong wind, an earthquake, and a fire, but the Lord instead chose to speak through "a gentle whisper" (1 Kings 19:12). And so, all those pastors who told me that God generally communicates with "a still small voice" were right. In fact, "gentle whisper" is translated as "a still small voice" in the King James Version. And more often than not, it seems God chooses to speak quietly, in our hearts.

While it might seem really spiritual to hear God speak loudly (it's always nice to have a fascinating story to tell other people), I eventually realized that sometimes the reason God speaks loudly to people is that they haven't been listening. Again, Paul provides a good example. Paul had no doubt heard the gospel before he had a vision of Christ on the road to Damascus and his subsequent conversion experience, because if he hadn't heard the gospel Christians were teaching, he wouldn't have been trying to arrest them. Until his encounter with Jesus, however, Paul resisted God's call to repentance and faith in Christ. As a result, the Lord spoke more clearly to Paul as he walked on the road to Damascus.

Similarly, I have listened to some Christians tell captivating stories of their call to engage in some particular type of ministry and how God made it abundantly clear through some miraculous event what they were supposed to do. In many cases, though, even before the miraculous event, the Lord had already spoken to these people about engaging in ministry, but because they were resisting God's guidance, God spoke loudly. Therefore, if God does choose to speak loudly to someone, it doesn't necessarily mean that person is more spiritual or more in tune with the Spirit than the next person.

God Is Speaking

Because God often speaks quietly, we don't always hear. Or perhaps the issue isn't so much that we don't hear God, but that we aren't always aware God is speaking. On numerous occasions I have listened to Christians ask, "Why isn't God talking to me? Why didn't the Lord answer me? Why can't I hear the Spirit right now? Why doesn't God answer me when I pray?" In the Bible, Job had similar questions. He suffered the loss of his family, wealth, health, possessions, and friends. And, like so many people in the midst of suffering, Job challenged God: "I cry out to you, God, but you do not answer; I stand up, but you merely look at me" (Job 30:20). Job also lamented, "Oh, that I had someone to hear me! I sign now my defense—let the Almighty answer me" (Job 31:35). Finally a response came:

Why do you complain to him [God] that he responds to no one's words? For God does speak—now one way, now another—though no one perceives it. In a dream, in a vision of the night, when deep sleep falls on people as they slumber in their beds, he may speak in their ears and terrify them with warnings. (Job 33:13–16)

Like Job, sometimes we are not aware of the ways God is speaking to us.[2] But if we learn to listen, we will hear them—or, better stated, we will be more aware of what we are hearing.

You've Already Heard God

The first time I remember hearing the Spirit speak to me was when I was nine years old. I sat in my hard pew one Sunday morning, listening to the guest preacher end his message. From behind the pulpit he asked if anyone would like to dedicate their lives to following Jesus. My heart thumped like the foot of a nervous rabbit. My Sunday-school teachers had asked my class the same thing on more than one occasion. But until that morning, I had determined that I would wait until I was older and had the chance to enjoy life awhile longer, that is, sin a little, before I would become a believer—maybe in my twenties, when it was time to get married.

That Sunday morning, however, the Spirit was urging me not to wait any longer. And so I bowed my head and prayed, "God, I want to live my life for Jesus." If you had a conversion experience similar in any way to mine, you have heard God speak. You might have even heard God speak by calling you to faith numerous times before you became a believer.

The biblical parable about a shepherd and his sheep illustrates the ability of believers to know the voice of God. Jesus said,

> Very truly I tell you Pharisees, anyone who does not enter the sheep pen by the gate, but climbs in by some other way, is a thief and a robber. The one who enters by the gate is the shepherd of the sheep. The gatekeeper opens the gate for him, and the sheep listen to his voice. He calls his own sheep by name and leads them out. When he has brought out all his own, he goes on ahead of them, and his sheep follow him because they know his voice. But they will never follow a stranger; in fact, they will run away from him because they do not recognize a stranger's voice. (John 10:1–5)

Jesus then explained the story: "I am the good shepherd. . . . My sheep listen to my voice; I know them, and they follow me" (vv. 11, 27). Jesus didn't say that his sheep *might* know his voice, but that they do "know his voice" (v. 4). In this story Jesus is first and foremost talking about salvation (vv. 9, 28). Therefore, if you are saved today, you have already responded to the Savior's voice. But the story doesn't only apply to salvation. Jesus didn't merely say that his sheep knew (past) his voice, but that they know (present) his voice.

Even though you might not think of yourself as someone who knows the Lord's voice, I suspect you have heard God in many ways.[3] Have you ever heard the Spirit speak through the Bible? Maybe a verse jumped out at you. When we read the Bible, we don't just ponder the things the Lord said "once upon a time," but we are confronted with the very voice of God speaking to us today. In times like this, the Scripture not only teaches about God and how we should live, but it also becomes a place where we encounter the living God.

Have you ever heard God speak to you through a sermon or during a time of worship? Have you ever felt a strong urge to pray for someone? Perhaps the Spirit has prompted you to encourage someone by sending them a note or phoning them. Has the Lord ever spoken to you about something you've done wrong or were about to do wrong? I am usually pretty good at hearing from God about my sin. Quite likely you have already heard the Spirit speak to you many times. You can even ask God right now: *When is the last time you spoke to me?*

Not What You Expect

One reason we aren't aware of the times God speaks to us is that when it happens, it isn't always what we might expect. Many students who come into my office only desire to hear the Lord's voice so God will help them make difficult life decisions, like what job to take or where to live, but they usually aren't so thrilled with hearing from the Spirit about the ways they need to stop sinning. God, however, doesn't want to be our free psychic hotline—God wants a close and personal relationship with us.

God may direct you regarding your future, but I've noticed that when God told a person in the Bible to go somewhere, they usually weren't seeking divine direction. Rather, the Lord just gave them direction. For example, Abraham (called Abram at the time) lived with his family in Harran for decades and likely anticipated living there for a long time. He didn't seem to have any reason to wonder about where to move next. And then, out of the blue, God told him, "Go from your country, your people and your father's household to the land I will show you" (Genesis 12:1). But God spoke to Abraham about more than just where to live. For example, God told Abraham, "Do not be afraid" (Genesis 15:1).

God speaks for all kinds of reasons. A couple of days after we buried our stillborn baby, God spoke to encourage my wife. It was Krista's first time returning to the grave after we buried Avery. As the van rolled up to the cemetery gate, a song started playing on the radio. Krista listened as the singer declared how God does not abandon us in our sorrow. And as the tears slid down her cheeks, the song assured her that God holds our tears.[4]

Krista then stood by Avery's grave, reflecting and praying. When she got back in the van, another song immediately began to play. It held her captive to that spot near the grave. Through that song, God reassured her again: even though we might feel alone, God holds us in our moments of suffering. And because God even cares for the flowers (Matthew 6:28–30) and the sparrows (Matthew 10:29–31), we can be sure that God will hold our tomorrows.[5] More than she needed direction for her future, that day Krista needed to hear the words she had heard so many times in Sunday school as a child: "He's got the whole world in his hands."

Sometimes the Lord may speak because you need correction. One time I was thinking about how ignorant somebody sounded, and God spoke to me by warning me not to be self-righteous about knowledge. Sometimes "the Spirit himself testifies with our spirit that we are God's children" (Romans 8:16). At times God may speak to assure you that even though God isn't going to change the difficult situation you are in, God's "grace is sufficient for you" (2 Corinthians 12:9). Other times, you may ask God a question, and God won't answer you. The Lord is not obliged to answer you or respond in the way you want.

Silence

Some people experience silence from God because they actually don't want to hear from God (Deuteronomy 18:16). Most Christians I come across who find God silent, however, truly do long to hear from God, yet for some reason they just aren't hearing anything. They are sometimes left feeling unspiritual and asking many questions. The problem is, we can't force the Lord to speak. If you are struggling and not hearing God speak for whatever reason, please know you are not alone. Many biblical authors struggled with times of silence from God too. David lamented, "Every day I call to you, my God, but you do not answer. Every night you hear my voice, but I find no relief" (Psalm 22:2, author's paraphrase). At times like this, it is important that we continue to declare our faith and trust to God, as David did in the next verse: "Yet you are holy, enthroned on the praises of Israel" (v. 3 NLT).

Even when we don't hear from God, we can be assured that the Lord is still at work in our lives, because "we know that in all things God works for the good of those who love him, who have been called according to his purpose" (Romans 8:28). If you are in a place where you are not currently hearing from God, consider asking God if there is a reason and what you can do about it. Perhaps God is using silence to get your attention.

Testing Content

Hopefully you are not experiencing silence from God. Hopefully you realize that you have heard and have been hearing the Spirit speak. Nevertheless, when you do hear from God, it won't always be clear that it is God speaking to you. Pretty much everyone I talk to about hearing from God agrees that you will sometimes need to discern if you are hearing from God or not, no matter how long you have been a Christian.

Some Christians get anxious about discerning whether they are hearing from God or the Devil. No believer wants to follow the Devil's voice. The negative result is that some people decide discerning the Spirit's voice is too difficult and, therefore, they choose to stop listening to God altogether. Not listening to the Lord, however, may be just as dangerous for our lives as listening to the Devil. We must remind ourselves that God does speak. And we need to have more confidence in God's ability to address us than in Satan's ability to deceive us.[6] Rather than giving up on hearing from God, we should "test everything; *hold fast* to what is good" (1 Thessalonians 5:21 NRSV).

Whenever we believe we are hearing from God, we should test the content of the message. This starts by comparing what we are hearing in our hearts to how God has spoken in the Bible. If what you have heard contradicts the

Scripture, you obviously have not heard from God. For example, the Spirit would not tell a person that because their spouse is ignoring them, it is okay to commit adultery; the Lord has already unambiguously condemned adultery in the Bible (Mark 10:19).

Group Discernment

Sometimes what you think you hear from God does not contradict anything from the Bible, but it still might not be from God. A story from the pastor of a church near Chicago, illustrates this point:

> In the early 1990s, I was in the process of recuperating from a time of burnout and over-commitment. At my lowest point during that season of extreme exhaustion—when I was emotionally fried—a business friend of mine from out of state made an offer for me to join his company. It was an exciting and lucrative offer, and I truly thought that God might be calling me to leave church work and re-enter the marketplace.
>
> I was quite confident that I had heard God's voice . . . Nothing in Scripture would prohibit me from going back to my original career in the marketplace. . . .
>
> Somewhat begrudgingly, I called together a few spiritual mentors and other people whose opinions and

perspectives I genuinely trust, and who understood my current state of exhaustion. I described the offer I was considering, then sat back and listened to their response. To a person, they said, " . . . you are in no condition right now to make such a sweeping decision about your future. Even if you believe that God is steering you in this direction, we implore you to wait three months and then reevaluate at that time."

I will forever be grateful that I heeded their wise advice. Within a couple of months I did get healthier, and I began to see things more clearly. As I fell in love with my ministry role once more, I realized how much I would have missed if I had gotten that one decision wrong.[7]

This story illustrates another important way to test the content of a message: discuss what you have heard with other people you trust within the Christian community. Often when people hear from God, they are reluctant to share it with others because they fear they are wrong. When you discuss with others, however, you can find encouragement, particularly if you conclude you have indeed heard from the Lord. Furthermore, it can save you heartache, if you discern that you haven't heard from God.

We see the principle of group discernment practiced in the Bible. Before Paul and Barnabas embarked on their first missionary journey, the Holy Spirit spoke to the church and told them to set Barnabas and Paul apart for their mission journey. Only after "*they* had fasted and prayed" did the church commission Paul and Barnabas (Acts 13:3). Paul and Barnabas did not make the decision to go out as missionaries by themselves. Rather, "they"—the church—concluded this was the right thing to do. Group discernment took place again during Paul's second missionary journey. Only Paul had a vision of a man in Macedonia calling to him for help, but it was the whole group of people traveling with him who concluded that God called them to go and preach in Macedonia (Acts 16:9–10).

Wisdom and Waiting

Friends can also help you discern if what you think you have heard from God is wise. Proverbs 12:15 teaches us that "the way of fools seems right to them, but the wise listen to advice." Even though the Bible often affirms the value of wisdom and seeking wise counsel (Proverbs 4:7; James 1:5), some people think one way to confirm that a message is from God is if it is *not* wise "from a human perspective." They usually quote Isaiah 55:8, where the Lord says, "My thoughts are not your thoughts, neither are your ways my ways," as though this scripture indicates a general rule about God's plans for us. The previous verse, however, clarifies that the manner in which the Lord's ways differ from human ways is that if "the wicked forsake their ways and . . . turn to the LORD," God "will have mercy on them" and even "freely pardon" them. In other words, the Lord's ways differ from people's ways because God will forgive freely. Therefore, when God says, "My ways are not your ways," it does *not* mean that God only desires things for us that seem unwise from a human perspective. It is possible that in some instances God may ask you to do something that seems unwise from some human perspectives, but this is not a general rule about how God works.

If God does ask you to do something that doesn't immediately seem wise, wait and see if God confirms it in another way. For example, one day I peered out my window through the blinds and found that an ambulance was parked across the road at my neighbor's house. Right then, God directed me to walk across the road and offer to pray for my neighbor. I didn't think it was wise. I thought I might just be getting in the way of the paramedics or my neighbor might think I was being nosy. Still, I sensed the Spirit telling me I should hike over and offer to pray. Nevertheless, I closed the blinds and went back to preparing supper. Of course, my young and curious children kept peeking out the living room window to see what was going on across the street. I kept thinking about what God had said and was even debating with God about it. Then, one of my daughters said, "You should go pray for them." I smiled. I put on my flip flops and walked across the street ready to pray because I knew God was gently confirming for me what the Spirit had already spoken to my heart.

Another important way to test the content of a message you believe you have heard from the Lord is to wait and see if the prompting from God lasts. Taking this time will allow you to discern if it was really God speaking to you, or if you just had a temporary desire or whim.

Recognizing God's Voice

To summarize the last few sections of this chapter, first, when you think you are hearing from God, you should test the content of the message against the Scripture. Second, you can ask trusted friends in the Christian community what they think about what you heard, including their thoughts about the wisdom of the idea. Third, you can wait to see if the prompting from God remains, being confirmed in other ways as well. Unfortunately, sometimes these tests regarding the content of the message don't always work—that is, they don't always help clarify things for you, or they aren't practical. For example, what if you are in a church service and you believe God is telling you to go pray for an individual right then and there? You know it is biblical to pray for other people, but it isn't practical to ask someone what they think about the idea, and you probably don't have the time to wait to see if the prompting from God lasts. Situations like this show the importance of not only testing the content of the message you think you hear but also learning to discern what God's voice sounds like when God speaks to you so you can recognize it in the future.

You might be frustrated with the suggestion that you need to learn to recognize God's voice, just as I was once frustrated with the idea that I need to listen better to hear God speak, as though God can't speak loudly. The problem, if we can call it a problem, is that when the Spirit speaks to your heart and mind, God doesn't promise to give you big, special, profound thoughts that will stand out radically from other thoughts you might have. You might expect that if God is going to communicate to you through a dream, for example, it won't be like a normal dream—it will be a *dream*-dream—that is, an out-of-the-ordinary, super-spectacular dream. But God's voice doesn't always stand out in a majestic way. It is encouraging, though, that just as you learn to recognize the voice of your friends on the phone, you can also learn to better recognize the voice of God.

When God does speak to people, they often write it off as something else. They might think, *That is just me*, or, *It must be what I ate last night.* When God spoke to Samuel, he didn't immediately recognize God's voice either. The Lord had called for Samuel, but Samuel figured it was Eli the priest calling him. After Samuel had made this mistake three times, Eli told him to respond to God: "Speak, LORD, for your servant is listening" (1 Samuel 3:9). You might think Samuel should have recognized God's voice, especially since it seems Samuel heard a literal, audible voice. But, like many people today, Samuel came up with another explanation for what he heard.

Is It God?

I have found that God speaks differently to different people, so you will have to discern how the Lord communicates with you. The primary way you can learn to recognize God's voice is by getting used to recognizing it over time as you confirm times when the Lord has indeed been speaking to you.

One way to do this is by considering the fruit or outcome of the particular voice or prompting you have followed. Does the voice lead you in a generally disruptive or peaceful direction? How does the voice affect your relationship with God? If the voice consistently leads you to hurt people or to bad outcomes, there is a good chance the voice you heard was not from God.

This is not to say God will only ask you to do things that will make your life better or easier. When the Israelites were in slavery in Egypt, the Lord directed Moses to confront Pharaoh and tell him to free the Israelites. Moses eventually obeyed, but Pharaoh responded by telling the Egyptian slave drivers to push the Israelites harder in their work of making bricks. Things got harder for Moses, too, because the Israelites blamed Moses for their hardship (Exodus 5:21–23). Despite this hardship, Moses was confident he had heard from God because God confirmed it to Moses through miraculous signs (Exodus 4:2–7). Moreover, the Lord's direction ultimately saved Moses and the Israelites through their mass exodus out of Egypt (Exodus 12:31–34).

In addition to considering the outcomes of following the voice you hear, when you think you are hearing from the Lord, it can also be beneficial to ask God who is speaking. If God can talk to you about other things, then God can certainly clarify for you if it is really God speaking. I remember asking God once, "Is that really you, God?" and the Lord responded quite plainly, "No way!"

Another helpful way to recognize God's voice is to begin by identifying ways you have already heard the Spirit speaking to you. I have found I am really good at hearing the Lord when God talks to me about sin in my life. Because I can recognize God's voice when God communicates to me in that way, I can also hear the Lord speaking to me in the same way, but about other things.

Practice Listening

If we are going to hear from God and recognize God's voice, we need to practice listening to God. Perhaps it would be better to say we need to take more time for our relationship with God. The Lord wants to have a relationship with us, not just to tell us fascinating things. And as we build our relationship with God, we recognize God's voice more. But listening means more than just spending time praying, if by praying we only mean *talking to* God. To hear God and grow in relationship with God, we must make room for a two-way conversation. We might even ask the Lord some questions.

Many Christians find that the main way they hear from God is through the Bible, so one way to practice listening to God is by starting there. As you read the Bible, don't just study it or read a devotional about it, but also ask if God has anything to tell you through it. And then take some time to listen to God. Sometimes I hear the Lord speaking to me as I am reading the Bible, and other times not until after I have finished reading and am praying about what I read.

We can also practice listening to the Lord for the sake of ministering to other people. God often speaks to us when we are already following God's will, and we know God desires us to "serve one another humbly in love" (Galatians 5:13). When I read the Bible, especially in the New Testament, I see that most of the times God speaks is for the purpose of directing people to minister to others. I'm not saying God will tell us everything we should do in ministry—God has already made clear much of what we are supposed to do, like giving to those in need—but sometimes God will give us more specific direction.

One day I had a layover in a big international airport. I already knew God is pleased when we share the gospel with people, but as I wandered around the airport, I invited God to direct me to someone. I sensed the Lord telling me to stroll over to where a young man was sitting in a row of seats, leafing through a book. I didn't want to be rude and disrupt him, but I sat down beside him anyhow. I noticed he was holding a book on the religions of the world. The fact that this young man was already thinking about religion and spirituality confirmed for me that it was indeed God speaking to me. I asked him where he was from and about the book he was reading, and we ended up having a lengthy conversation. By the time I walked away, he said he was going to give the church he grew up in another try.

Reengage

If you've given up on hearing from God because you have been turned off by others who have made false claims about hearing God's voice, I encourage you to reengage God. No doubt you will also sometimes be wrong about hearing from God. I have been. But that is okay. We make all kinds of mistakes while learning math, and, while those mistakes can be frustrating, sometimes *very* frustrating, they are just part of the learning process. In the same way, over time you can learn to recognize God's voice better. I believe the Lord would say to some of you today what God said to Jeremiah: "Call to me and I will answer you and tell you great and unsearchable things you do not know" (Jeremiah 33:3).

Thank you, Lord, that you are not silent, but you speak to us by the Holy Spirit. Please help us become more aware of when you are speaking to us. Help us also obey when we do hear your voice. Forgive us for any times we have turned you into a psychic hotline. Help us aim for intimacy with you instead.

Questions for Reflection or Discussion

1. Do you get more frustrated or excited at the prospect of hearing the Spirit speak?
2. Has anything in this chapter led you to change your thinking about how God speaks or what God might speak to you about?
3. What are some ways and reasons God has spoken to you in the past?
4. Has God ever spoken to you at a time when you weren't asking God anything?
5. If someone came to you and said, "I think God might be speaking to me about something," how would you help that person discern whether they were hearing from God?

CHAPTER 4

CRAZY TALK?

Praying in Tongues

CRAZY TALK?

We leaned against the wall in the bathroom, trying to sort out the new experience my friend had just had in the service. He had a *what just happened?* look on his face and a twinkle in his eye. And he was grinning like he'd just found a twenty-dollar bill on the ground. He was asking the kinds of questions most people ponder when they first speak in tongues. *Is it just me? Can I speak in tongues again? Am I crazy?* It makes sense that he was asking such questions because the experience can seem peculiar. For those who aren't from a Pentecostal or Charismatic background, tongues are sometimes viewed as nothing more than unintelligent noises those "crazy" charismatics make because they don't know any better. At least this is a little more charitable than accusing people who speak in tongues of being demon possessed! Even those who speak in tongues can feel strange and nervous about it. And they might not want others to hear them doing it. After all, some weird Christians speak in tongues, and we certainly don't want to be like *them*.

Many people from back in the days of the New Testament also experienced a sense of uncertainty when they heard others speaking in tongues. On the day of Pentecost, a group of believers was baptized in the Holy Spirit and they "began to speak in other tongues" (Acts 2:4). Some who heard them were "amazed and perplexed" (Acts 2:12). Others made fun of them and accused them of being drunk, saying, "They have had too much wine" (Acts 2:13). It seems the apostle Paul also encountered adverse reactions to speaking in tongues because he warned the Corinthians that when people are doing this, others might accuse them of being "out of [their] mind" (1 Corinthians 14:23).

A Bad Reputation

Beyond the adverse reaction people might have when other people speak in tongues, some Christians have become antagonistic to the practice because of the way certain Christians have treated those who haven't spoken tongues. A friend of mind told me about his grandparents who were required to sit in the back pew at their Pentecostal church because they didn't speak in tongues. Another friend of mine explained how she was pressured to speak in tongues when she attended church camp as a child. As some leaders were praying for her to be filled with the Spirit and to speak in tongues, they encouraged her by declaring that they were willing to stay in the chapel to pray all day and all night until she was filled with the Spirit. She wasn't too thrilled with this prospect—she wanted to get out of the chapel service and back to the rest of the campers before it was time to go to the canteen. So she faked it. And then she skipped away from the chapel service with the camp counselors praising God behind her. Such experiences don't inspire people to be open to the practice of praying in tongues.

The practice has also developed a bit of a bad reputation because of some seemingly critical comments the apostle Paul made regarding it. In 1 Corinthians 14 Paul warned that when people speak in tongues, "no one understands them" (v. 2) and that, as a result, no one can say, "Amen," in response (v. 16). He also emphasized that he would rather have the Corinthians prophesy than speak in tongues (v. 5), because when a person speaks in tongues, others are not encouraged or strengthened (v. 17). Beyond this, Paul described speaking in tongues as "speaking into the air" (v. 9), and he stressed, "In the church I would rather speak five intelligible words to instruct others than ten thousand words in a tongue" (v. 19).

When we read all the cautions Paul gave regarding speaking in tongues, we have to remember that he wrote 1 Corinthians as a letter to a dysfunctional church. When I remember this, I realize the New Testament years were not always "the good old days." Besides the sexual immorality present in the Corinthian church (1 Corinthians 5:1–5 and chapter 6), believers there were arguing with each other (1:11). To encourage church unity, Paul emphasized that the church was gathered together by the Spirit to function as the body of Christ (12:12–27). And Paul reminded them that they—the church—were a temple of the Holy Spirit that must not be destroyed (3:16–17). The Corinthian church was divided over the use of spiritual gifts, and speaking in tongues in particular. So Paul tried to encourage church unity among the Corinthians by writing to them about the correct use of spiritual gifts. We read about this in 1 Corinthians chapters 12 and 14.

Once we understand that Paul was writing to correct and even rebuke certain *abuses* among the Corinthians, it becomes easy to understand why he said so many things that seem critical about speaking in tongues. Nevertheless, in the midst of this, he also expressed a sense of joy about the practice, when it happens appropriately: "I would like every one of you to speak in tongues" (1 Corinthians 14:5), he declared; and also, "*I thank God* that I speak in tongues more than all of you" (v. 18). Beyond just speaking in tongues, Paul also practiced the joy of singing in tongues (v. 15). This might be what he had in mind when he wrote about "spiritual songs" (Ephesians 5:19 ESV).

Praying in Tongues

In this chapter I focus specifically on praying in tongues, but people can speak in tongues in another way: namely, the gift of tongues accompanied by interpretation, which sometimes happens in a congregational worship setting. Paul himself made a distinction between a person praying in tongues and a person giving a message in tongues for a congregation: "I thank God that I speak in tongues more than all of you. *But in the church* I would rather speak five intelligible words to instruct others than ten thousand words in a tongue" (1 Corinthians 14:18–19). We see in these two verses a contrast between his practice of praying in tongues and his speaking "in the church." Earlier in the chapter, Paul explicitly referred to praying in tongues when he said, "If I pray in a tongue . . ." (v. 14). We also find numerous instances of praying in tongues throughout the book of Acts, times where there was no expectation that tongues needed interpretation.[1] This experience of praying in tongues—what some people refer to as a prayer language or spiritual language—is my focus in this chapter.

You may be thinking, *There isn't much in the Bible about tongues. How can this book I'm reading have a whole chapter on the topic?* In fact there is a fair amount in the Bible about speaking in tongues—much more than, for example, the virgin birth of Jesus Christ found only in

Matthew 1:23 and Luke 1:27 and 34, a doctrine that the church has held for centuries.

People occasionally make a number of errors when it comes to thinking about praying in tongues. Most important, these mistakes can easily hinder people from valuing the experience and, as a result, might keep them from wanting to speak in tongues.

Error 1: Tongues Are Only a Sign of Spirit Baptism

If you read the book of Acts, you will see a clear connection between speaking in tongues and being baptized in the Spirit (Acts 2:4; 10:46; 19:6). As a result, some Christians have concluded that tongues are the initial evidence of being baptized in the Spirit—that is, that tongues are a key indicator of a person having been baptized in the Spirit. Whether or not this conclusion is correct, the way some have emphasized this connection between tongues and Spirit baptism has actually (and ironically) caused some people to pray in tongues less. They reason that if tongues are only a sign of Spirit baptism, all a person has to do is speak in tongues once and he or she can stop, since tongues are presumably nothing more than proof of a previous experience. In this sense, tongues can become something like a diploma that tells you, "I once went to college, but now I'm done studying—and I don't need to speak in tongues anymore." Again, the problem with thinking that tongues is *only* a sign of being baptized in the Holy Spirit is that, first of all, there is no reason to expect that speaking in tongues could be an enduring spiritual practice for a believer, beyond that first instance. This would also mean praying in tongues has no meaning or value by itself, because the purpose of praying in tongues would then only be to point to something else, that is, Spirit baptism. In reality, there is much more to Spirit baptism than praying in tongues, and the gift of tongues is more than just a sign of Spirit baptism.

Error 2: Tongues Are Just for a Few People

People often mistakenly think speaking in tongues is only for a few people. It is easy to understand why someone might think this. For starters, in 1 Corinthians 12 and 14, Paul referred to speaking in tongues as a "gift." If it is a gift, wouldn't we think only the gifted would be able to speak in tongues? The answer might seem to be yes. And this conclusion might find further support in Paul's questions at the end of 1 Corinthians 12, where he asked, "Are all apostles? Are all prophets? Are all teachers? Do all work miracles? Do all have gifts of healing? Do all speak in tongues? Do all interpret?" (vv. 29–30). Paul's implied answer to all these questions was, "No, not everyone is an apostle, not everyone teaches, does miracles . . . or speaks in tongues." And this is true. The Spirit gives people different gifts. At the same time, if we read this passage closely, it becomes clear that when Paul implied that not everyone speaks in tongues, he did not have in mind the more general practice of praying in tongues. Rather, he was saying more specifically that not everyone has the gift of speaking in tongues *for a church congregation*, a gift that is *followed by the gift of interpretation*. This does not mean, however, that only a few people (the gifted) can pray in tongues.

Considering a few other gifts of the Spirit makes this apparent. Paul referred to "gifts of healing, of helping, of guidance, and of different kinds of tongues" (1 Corinthians 12:28). Like Paul, we can ask, "Do all have gifts of healing?" (v. 30). And the answer would be no. Yet, God can use any praying Christian to heal somebody. Similarly, we can ask, "Do all have the gift of helping others?" Again, the answer would be no. But I sure hope that when I am in a pinch, anyone has the ability to help me, even if they don't think they are "gifted." The same could be said about the gift of encouragement, the gift of giving, and other gifts (Romans 12:8). If only those with the gift of giving can give, pastors might as well quit passing the offering plate on Sunday morning. If some have the gift of prophecy, and yet "you can all prophesy in turn" (1 Corinthians 14:31), it becomes clear that, similarly, some can have the gift of tongues for a congregation, but anyone can potentially speak in tongues as they pray. This makes sense of Paul's warning about times when "the whole church comes together and *everyone* speaks in tongues" (v. 23). It also makes sense for Paul to have written, "I would like every one of you to speak in tongues" (v. 5).

Errors 3 and 4: It's Magical or It's "Just Me"

A third error some people make regarding praying in tongues is thinking that because the Spirit is involved, tongues are a magical thing we have no control over. One person told me she wasn't going to speak in tongues until God made her do it. She expected God to basically pry her mouth open and magically move her tongue and force sounds to come out of her mouth. People like this wait in silence, saying nothing, supposing that a miracle will eventually take place.

From a completely opposite perspective, when the friend I mentioned in the beginning of this chapter spoke in tongues for the first time, he wondered if it was "just him." That is, he questioned if he was only making up senseless sounds. Likewise, some people who haven't spoken in tongues think tongues are just gibberish.

Let's try something. Say this really fast a few times: "He bought a Honda. She bought a Hyundai. Could have bought a Kia. Should have bought a Ford." You probably sound like you are praying in tongues, but really all that you are doing is buying cars. Similarly, when I jump out from behind a corner and try to scare my young daughters by yelling, "Hucka-ba-lucka!" I am still not speaking in tongues. Once one engages in speaking in tongues enough, it becomes clear that not just any noises equate to tongues.

One summer as I was counseling children at a church camp, the leaders of the camp taught about being filled with the Spirit and speaking in tongues. At the end of one evening message, they invited children to walk to the front of the muggy sanctuary to be prayed for. Two young boys scampered to the stage and then sat facing one another on the stairs. One looked at his friend and said, "Repeat after me," and then he proceeded to teach his friend a few noises that resembled what he heard when others had spoken in tongues. As innocent as this was, it wasn't speaking in tongues because it isn't just any noises we make.

Synergy with the Spirit

When we genuinely pray in tongues, God is involved. As Paul said, those "who speak in a tongue . . . utter mysteries by the Spirit" (1 Corinthians 14:2). So it isn't "just me." But at the same time, tongues are not a magical thing I have no control over. Rather, the truth is somewhere in the middle.

I am involved when I pray in tongues, and God is also involved. A synergy of sorts occurs. The Spirit is involved, yet Paul could say, "*I speak in tongues*" (v. 18) and "*I will pray*" in tongues (v. 15). In other words, we can decide to pray in tongues even though the Spirit enables us. Or perhaps I should say, because the Spirit enables us.

I have heard stories from some Christians who have had experiences when they felt like they had no choice but to speak in tongues. But, more often than not, when people pray in tongues they experience their spirit working together with the Spirit of God. Frank Macchia's testimony of the first time he spoke in tongues illustrates this: "I felt a fountain well up within me. It grew stronger and stronger until it burst forth with great strength. I began to pray in tongues. It was not forced, neither from me nor from God. In fact, it seemed at the moment to be the most natural thing to do."[2] As with this example, most people who pray in tongues affirm that they still have good control over themselves while speaking in tongues. Paul's instructions to the Corinthians to take turns and limit the amount of speaking in tongues in a church gathering also presupposes that people have some control over when they might speak in tongues (1 Corinthians 14:27–28, 32). The Spirit usually does not force one to speak in tongues. Rather, speaking in tongues occurs through a synergy as the Spirit enables people to pray in tongues.

Unfruitful?

In the midst of 1 Corinthians 14, Paul said something seemingly negative about tongues when he revealed that his "mind is unfruitful" when he prayed in tongues (v. 14). For many people in today's scientifically and technologically advanced societies, doing something where our minds are considered unfruitful doesn't sound positive. Nevertheless, just because a person's mind is unfruitful as they pray in tongues doesn't mean praying in tongues as a whole is an unproductive exercise. We human beings are more than just minds. When a person prays in tongues, they can say, "My spirit prays" (v. 14). Even though Paul's mind was unfruitful as he prayed in tongues, he didn't limit prayer to a language he knew. Instead, Paul reasoned, "So what shall I do? I will pray with my spirit, but I will also pray with my understanding" (v. 15).

As someone prays in tongues, they may not understand what they are praying about, and their mind may be unfruitful, but this does not mean it is meaningless or *irrational* prayer. Rather, praying in tongues is a *supra-rational* experience—that is, an experience that goes beyond our understanding and rationality. Many other experiences in life might be described as being above rationality. A person can communicate sorrow or pain through weeping in a way words cannot express. One might convey joy through dancing or jumping up and down. Through a painting or sculpture, an artist can express thoughts and emotions that go beyond words. Likewise, sometimes people feel the need to express themselves to God by clapping, or kneeling, or raising their hands. At other times people respond to God's presence with reverent silence. Some have also had an experience where they sense the presence of the Holy Spirit and start weeping. When asked, they can't quite explain why they are crying, but they know God is doing a deep work in their heart. As in each of these supra-rational experiences, as people pray in tongues, the Spirit helps them express things to God that the mind alone is unable to put into words. Their minds may be unfruitful, but their prayers are not.

Praise, Thanksgiving, and Edification

Sometimes when people pray in tongues, they "are praising God in the Spirit" (1 Corinthians 14:16). Thus, when people spoke in tongues on the day of Pentecost, the Bible says they were "declaring the wonders of God" (Acts 2:11). When people pray in tongues, it is also possible that they "are giving thanks" to God (1 Corinthians 14:17). I can certainly say that many times I have been in a worship service or praying on my own when exclaiming, "Praise you, God!" or, "Thank you, Jesus!" just doesn't seem to be enough. At times like this I often choose to praise God in tongues.

Praying in tongues can also be edifying, for "anyone who

83

speaks in a tongue edifies themselves" (1 Corinthians 14:4). Paul continued by cautioning, "but the one who prophesies edifies the church." I will remind you once again that Paul only wrote the last part of this verse because he was correcting the Corinthians. When someone speaks in tongues, "no one understands them" (v. 2), and because of this, if a person goes to church and prays in tongues all the time, it isn't going to benefit others at the church. Similarly, if I wrote this book in tongues (if that were possible), it would not be helpful. I can certainly understand Paul's concern. I would rather write "five intelligible words to instruct others than ten thousand words in a tongue" (v. 19).

While noting Paul's desire that the Corinthians edify one another in church, we must be careful not to miss where he affirmed some value in tongues, for "anyone who speaks in a tongue edifies themselves" (1 Corinthians 14:4). But what does it mean to edify? I don't remember the last time I arrived home from work and said to my wife, "Hi, honey. What a great day. I was really edified today." The Greek word translated *edify* (*oikodomē*) means "to promote growth or to build up [like building or repairing a house]." So when you need to be built up or repaired—some people call this inner healing—that can be a time to pray in tongues. Romans 8:6 reminds us that "the mind governed by the Spirit is life and peace." This can come about as you edify yourself by praying in tongues.

Another Form of Prayer

Overall, praying in tongues is another form of prayer; Christians can "pray in a tongue" (1 Corinthians 14:15). And just as you can pray about anything in a language you know, you might pray about anything in tongues. Sometimes you might have desires and prayers you just can't express with words. Praying in tongues can help you express those feelings to God. Or you could be praying for yourself or for another person and not know how to pray, but the Spirit might help you by enabling you to pray in tongues. One advantage of doing this is that as the Spirit prays through you, your prayers won't be selfish or out of order because "the Spirit intercedes for God's people in accordance with the will of God" (Romans 8:27).

Praying in tongues can also serve as a means of building your relationship with God. It is no secret that, in general, prayer is foundational to intimacy with God. This is why "Jesus often withdrew to lonely places and prayed" (Luke 5:16). Like other forms of prayer, when I pray in tongues, I am doing more than just giving requests to God—I am having communion with God. Therefore, praying in tongues is important not only because of the things I am saying, but also because of what God is doing through me and in relationship with me.[3] Whenever I pray in tongues, my spirit is engaged with or immersed in God's Spirit. To use Paul's words, my "*spirit* prays" (1 Corinthians 14:14), but I also "utter mysteries by the *Spirit*" (v. 2). In this type of praying, you can grow in your relationship with God.

Encouragement

If you are someone who has already spoken in tongues, I hope I have encouraged you to make praying in tongues a regular part of your relationship with God. When I was a teenager, I prayed in tongues fairly regularly, but over time I started to get a little cynical regarding the practice. My cynicism was not really a result of the gift of tongues itself, but of certain people who spoke in tongues. I had come across a number of people who prayed in tongues but who didn't seem to exhibit much of the fruit of the Spirit (Galatians 5). Others seemed insincere as they prayed in tongues. I remember one evening when I watched someone in a prayer meeting wander back and forth through the room, praying in tongues. As he walked he was gazing around at other people like he was out for a stroll through the neighborhood. I figured he wasn't actually praying to God—he was just making some noise, like "a resounding gong or a clanging cymbal" (1 Corinthians 13:1). As a result of experiences like this, although I didn't completely quit praying in tongues, the practice began to lose importance for me.

A number of experiences, though, renewed my perspective on praying in tongues. For example, I remember when I was working in a church and my office was next to another pastor's office. Every once in a while, the other pastor would crank up the music in his office and worship God. And, quite often, he would pray in tongues. While this was sometimes a little distracting, on more than one occasion I could so feel the presence of God that I had to stop what I was doing on my computer and, unbeknownst to the other pastor, I would join him in worshipping and praising God in tongues. The fact that the other pastor sat alone in his office helped me overcome my cynicism. He was not putting on a show for the church congregation. He was not praying in tongues so people could see him acting spiritual in the prayer room. He was just being authentic in his relationship with God. Moments like this have encouraged me to realize that even if some people seem to be "a resounding gong or a clanging cymbal" when they speak in tongues, I can still find great value in the practice.

How to Speak in Tongues

My desire for everyone who reads this chapter is the same as Paul's: "I would like every one of you to speak in tongues" (1 Corinthians 14:5). Nevertheless, I know some people will read this who have not yet spoken in tongues. You might think, *I'm not spiritual enough*. Or, *I'm too weak. I could never speak in tongues*. I've got good news for you! If you feel this way, you are actually an excellent candidate to pray in tongues so you, too, can be edified, or built up, through the experience. It is encouraging to remember that the New Testament described both mature Christians (like Paul) and immature Christians (like the Corinthians) who spoke in tongues. Perfection is not a requirement.

You may be wondering, then, *How do I speak in tongues?* I wish there were an easy answer to this. Despite what some books and pastors might say, I do not see a formula in Scripture that explains how to speak in tongues. Sometimes someone might lay hands and pray for a person before the person starts praying in tongues (Acts 19:6), but not always (Acts 10:44–46). Sometimes it happens in a prayer meeting (Acts 2:1–4), and other times it doesn't. It can happen in different places, in different ways.

Nevertheless, I do see at least two principles in the Bible that might help you receive the ability to pray in tongues. First, the Bible teaches us to "eagerly desire gifts of the Spirit" (1 Corinthians 14:1). In most cases, God is not going to give you a gift that you do not truly want. This includes speaking in tongues. I know someone who sat on his hands while he was in a church service because he was sure that if he raised his hands in worship to God, he was going to start speaking in tongues.

A second principle for gaining the ability to pray in tongues is to ask God to give you the ability. Jesus said,

> Which of you, if your son asks for bread, will give him a stone? Or if he asks for a fish, will give him a snake? If you, then, though you are evil, know how to give good gifts to your children, how much more will your Father in heaven give good gifts to those who ask him! (Matthew 7:9–11)

The gospel of Luke shares the same story and relates the "good gifts" that the Father gives specifically to the Holy Spirit: "How much more will your Father in heaven give the Holy Spirit to those who ask him!" (Luke 11:13). Even if you have asked God more than once to enable you to pray in tongues, I encourage you to keep asking.

First Experiences

I have heard many stories from individuals about their first experience praying in tongues, and all are different. Sometimes they were in a prayer meeting, other times they were at home alone. When I first spoke in tongues, I was in a church service standing at the front of the sanctuary worshipping God after an altar call. As I stood there with my hands raised and my eyes closed, someone approached me and asked me if I wanted to be filled with the Spirit. I wasn't too sure what he meant, but it sounded good, so I responded affirmatively. He lead me in a prayer: "God, I ask you to now baptize me in the Spirit." I thought this meant being slain in the Spirit, so I let myself fall backward. He was kind enough to catch me. (Give me a break—I was a teenager.) As I lay there on the cold, musty carpet, I somehow realized that Spirit baptism wasn't the same as being slain in the Spirit. I think I prayed the prayer again. Then, after a little while, I started to speak in tongues. My mouth didn't feel any different than normal; I just didn't understand the words I was saying.

In 1906, Ellen Hebden and her husband started what eventually became the first Pentecostal church in Canada, and she was probably the first Canadian to speak in tongues during the contemporary Pentecostal-Charismatic movement. This is how Ellen described what happened to her in Toronto on November 17, 1906:

> That day I had done quite a lot of visiting in connection with the mission, and, being very tired, I retired at 10:10 p.m. Only a short time elapsed when the Spirit of God prompted me to rise and pray, which I immediately did. For some months I had been seeking earnestly for more power to heal the sick, and with this desire still in my heart I began to pray. . . . My whole being seemed to

be filled with praise and adoration such as I had never realized before. . . . Then God began speaking to me . . . and a very quiet yet distinct voice said, "Tongues." I said, "No, Lord, not Tongues." Then followed a moment of deathlike stillness, when the voice again uttered the word "Tongues." This time I felt afraid of grieving the Lord and I said, "Tongues, or anything that will please Thee and bring glory to Thy name." One unknown word was repeated several times and I thought that must be Tongues.[4]

Ellen's story is different from mine, and, if you haven't yet spoken in tongues, your first experience likely will be different from ours. But if you do find yourself praying and you sense God is leading you to pray in tongues, let that first sound out, and the Spirit will guide you. A mouth that is glued shut will get you nowhere. Remember, a synergy happens: *you* pray in tongues, and the *Spirit* enables you. You will no doubt wonder if it is "just me," but remember what Jesus said—the Father won't give you a stone if you ask for bread.

Tongues and Spirituality

I have come to value speaking in tongues as a regular part of my prayer life, so it saddens me when people reject the experience. We should "not forbid speaking in tongues" (1 Corinthians 14:39). At the same time, we must be careful not to make this experience the pinnacle of spirituality. Remember, there is a long history of both immature Christians and mature Christians who have spoken in tongues. Plus, it is always a sobering reminder that "if I speak in the tongues of men or of angels, but do not have love, I am only a resounding gong or a clanging cymbal" (1 Corinthians 13:1). And so, like the apostle Paul, I will continue to "pray with my spirit, but I will also pray with my understanding; I will sing with my spirit, but I will also sing with my understanding" (1 Corinthians 14:15).

Father, forgive us if we have ever viewed tongues as more important than other aspects of being in relationship with you. When we do not know how or what to pray, may your Spirit guide our prayers, even prayers in tongues. May your Spirit build us up and help us to praise you well.

Questions for Reflection or Discussion

1. Have you ever believed one of the four errors this chapter describes about speaking in tongues?
2. If you have prayed in tongues, what value do you find in it as a regular spiritual practice?
3. If you have prayed in tongues, how did it first happen and what was the experience like?

4. If you have never prayed in tongues, how open are you to the Spirit praying through you in this way?

5. Why do you suppose that the Bible does not regard speaking in tongues as the pinnacle of one's spirituality?

CHAPTER 5

LIVING LARGE

*Faith, Health, Wealth, and
Other Wonderful Things*

Jim slouched on his hospital bed as the doctor informed him there was nothing more she could do to help him. After she left the room, he stared at the ceiling and cried out to the Great Physician, the heavenly Father who "heals all your diseases" (Psalm 103:3). Not willing to accept defeat, Jim stood up and shuffled over to the bathroom. He looked deep into the mirror and confidently confessed the healing power of the Holy Spirit over his life. And he claimed the truth of Scripture. He recited texts like Proverbs 12:21: "No harm overtakes the righteous." And he quoted Isaiah 53:5: "But he was pierced for our transgressions, he was crushed for our iniquities; the punishment that brought us peace was upon him, and by his wounds we are healed."

Jim said he could not see his healing with his physical eyes, but that he looked for it with his spiritual eyes. He claimed his healing. And, eventually . . . he received it! As wonderful as it is that Jim was healed, before we cheer too loudly for this story, we should pause and consider what it means to have faith in God and how God responds to our faith.

The idea that we can claim a spiritual reality in spite of our physical reality comes out of what many refer to as the prosperity gospel, the health-and-wealth gospel, word-faith theology, or simply, the faith movement. The prosperity gospel comes in different shapes and sizes, but at the heart of it is the teaching that God desires all Christians to prosper in every aspect of their lives. While this includes things like having healthy relationships, those who teach some version of prosperity theology usually emphasize financial and physical health. One wonders if the health and wealth gospel blesses the American dream as if it came from God. On the financial side of things, the emphasis on prosperity can be problematic—at its best it rightly encourages us to trust in God as our provider, whereas at its worst the prosperity gospel blesses selfish greed (1 Timothy 6:9)—but in this chapter I focus particularly on the issue of healing.

Who Teaches This?

It is not always easy to know if you are listening to a pastor who teaches the prosperity gospel or not. First of all, those who preach health and wealth generally hold to the same orthodox theology as the whole of the evangelical church—in other words, they have a lot of biblical things to say, including emphasizing that Jesus is Savior. Second, since people usually speak of "prosperity gospel" with scorn, when asked outright, many pastors will deny they believe in the prosperity gospel, even when they preach prosperity from the pulpit. One such pastor from Florida said, "I'm not one of those who would be called a prosperity preacher . . . I believe in prosperity. I believe in the blessing of God. But typically, a prosperity preacher [makes it] their life's message. I don't feel like it's my life message, but it's part of the Message, the Word of God."[1]

Even when people are hesitant to identify themselves with the prosperity gospel, you can often recognize prosperity teachers by their words. Typically, you will notice an emphasis on health or wealth. For example, one prominent author claimed, "When you are walking in the Word of God, you will prosper and be in *health*."[2] Another famous preacher emphasized, "You are destined to reign in life. You are called by the Lord to be a success, to enjoy *wealth*, to enjoy *health*, and to enjoy a life of victory. It is not the Lord's desire that you live a life of defeat, poverty, and failure. He has called you to be the head and not the tail."[3]

Not everyone who teaches the prosperity gospel will be quite so explicit and easy to recognize, however, in part because different preachers will emphasize prosperity in varying degrees, and they may emphasize only one of the central themes: either health or wealth. Nevertheless, you can listen for key phrases to help you recognize if you might be in the presence of a prosperity teacher. People who follow this teaching sometimes speak of releasing their faith, speaking their faith, and believing God *for* things. As an expression of these ideas, they might also speak of declaring or confessing certain things over their lives. For example, if you are asked to "declare that this will be your year of . . . (fill in the blank)," there is a good chance you are in the presence of someone who either teaches or has been strongly influenced by those who hold to the prosperity gospel.

Historians often point to Kenneth Hagin Sr. (1917–2003) as the father of the faith movement, although the teachings clearly go back to men like E. W. Kenyon (1867–1948), A. A. Allen (1911–1970), and Oral Roberts (1918–2009). You can find some prosperity preachers, often only tolerated, within denominations, usually Pentecostal or Charismatic, but most are found in independent churches or in loose networks of churches that share the prosperity message as an important theme. Although they all present the properity gospel in their own way and include their own distinct emphases, famous pastors and speakers who are often identified as prosperity teachers include Kenneth Copeland, Fred Price, Benny Hinn, Joel Osteen, Creflo Dollar, Guillermo Maldonado, Paula White, T. D. Jakes, Charles Capps, John Hagee, Rod Parsley, Paul Morton, Eddie Long, Jesse Duplantis, Jerry Savelle, Miles Munroe, Morris Cerullo, Jim Bakker, Joyce Meyer, and Joseph Prince. Other well-known personalities could also be named, not to mention those in smaller churches without fame.[4]

The Good, the Bad, and the Ugly

I have mentioned names so that you can be aware of some places where prosperity teachings are found, but not to discredit everything that takes place in the ministries these teachers lead. To the contrary, I'm sure all the people listed above have been used by God in various ways, from seeing people healed to helping people come to faith in Christ. And at least some aspects of their preaching and teaching are worth commending. Kenneth Hagin, for example, rightly encourages readers to "meditate on the Word. Dig deeply into it. Feed upon it."[5] And those who promote the prosperity gospel do well to actually expect that God is going to work in their lives, whereas many Christians today really don't expect much from God. As Gordon Fee, a critic of the health and wealth gospel, observed, "Most Christians' expectation level, when it comes to the miraculous, is somewhere between zero and minus five."[6]

Yet overall, the health and wealth gospel is problematic and even dangerous. Prosperity preachers generally take Scripture out of context when attempting to build a biblical case for the health and wealth gospel. I point readers to Gordon Fee's book, *The Disease of the Health and Wealth Gospels,* for a helpful analysis. With healing in particular, those who proclaim the health and wealth gospel are correct to emphasize that Jesus healed many people and that God still heals people today. It becomes problematic, however, when teachers claim that (1) there is some sort of an automatic connection between our level of faith and receiving healing from God, and (2) one way to exercise your faith is by claiming your healing through positive confession.

Faith and Healing

A friend of mine lost her husband to cancer when they were still young in their marriage. Some people accused them of lacking faith when he wasn't getting better. Aside from their poor understanding of Scripture, this wasn't a loving response to a suffering couple.

And yet, faith is instrumental in healing. There were a few times that Jesus said to someone, "Your faith has healed you" (Mark 10:52). So, sometimes it is the faith of the sick person that is instrumental in healing. Sometimes, however, it is the faith of the person praying that seems to matter more. James 5:15 highlights how "the prayer offered in faith will make the sick person well." If the people who were discouraging my friends had followed their own logic that a certain amount of faith was necessary for a person to be healed, then, to be fair, they also should have been apologizing that they didn't have enough faith when they were praying for my friend's husband and that it was, perhaps, their own fault that he wasn't being healed. Of course, people who think that a certain amount of faith is necessary for healing are usually quicker to point their fingers at others than to point back at themselves.

The fact of the matter is that no person's faith—neither the faith of the sick person nor the faith of the person praying—guarantees healing in this life. Even those who do experience healing will eventually no longer be healed, at which point they will die. Those with faith will—praise the Lord—all experience ultimate healing, or "the redemption of our bodies" (Romans 8:23), in the future at the resurrection. But in this life, healing is never a guarantee. The Bible instructs us to pray for healing and, because God is compassionate and all-powerful, we can expect God will heal some people. Nevertheless, regardless of how holy a person is, how hard a person prays, or how much faith one may have, miracles do not always come. Realizing this would save many people a lot of grief.

Surely the apostle Paul was a man of great faith. Paul not only did miracles, but the Bible says that "God did *extraordinary* miracles through Paul" (Acts 19:11). And yet, Paul himself was not always healed. Paul reminded the Galatians that "it was because of an illness that I first preached the gospel to you" (Galatians 4:13). And he also had sick friends for whom he had no doubt prayed. To Timothy, he wrote that he left "Trophimus sick in Miletus" (2 Timothy 4:20), and in Philippians we learn that Paul's friend Epaphroditus was so sick that he "almost died" (2:27). Paul nowhere suggested that these people were sick because he or they were lacking faith. And he didn't tell Timothy that Timothy needed to exercise more faith because of his "frequent illness" (1 Timothy 5:23). Instead, he suggested a medicinal remedy. Suffering through sickness is not a sure sign of a lack of faith. Indeed, as Larry Hart rightly observed, "It takes *greater* faith to continue trusting, thanking, praising, and serving the Lord when the healing doesn't come as we desire."[7]

Faith and Prosperity

If you stop and think about faith more widely, you will realize that faith does not guarantee a life of prosperity, for faith does not guarantee a good life in general. You can probably think of someone from your church who is a great example of faith, yet who has had to endure significant experiences of suffering. Aside from Jesus, who was murdered despite his close relationship with the Father, the book of Hebrews contains a faith "hall of fame" celebrating the lives of many faith-filled people who endured much hardship. Hebrews 11 presents people like Noah, Abraham, Isaac, and Jacob as people who "were still living by faith when they died," and yet, we are reminded that "they did not receive the things promised" (v. 13). The writer added stories of people like Joseph, Moses, and Rahab. Some of these heroes were people "who through faith conquered kingdoms, administered justice, and gained what was promised; who shut the mouths of lions, quenched the fury of the flames, and escaped the edge of the sword; whose weakness was turned to strength; and who became powerful in battle and routed foreign armies. Women received back their dead, raised to life again" (vv. 33–35). Yes! The life of faith!

We can be tempted to stop reading the chapter there, but Hebrews 11 continues, "There were others who were tortured, refusing to be released so that they might gain an even better resurrection. Some faced jeers and flogging, and even chains and imprisonment. They were put to death by stoning; they were sawed in two; they were killed by the sword. They went about in sheepskins and goatskins, destitute, persecuted and mistreated" (vv. 35–37). These outcomes don't sound desirable. This is certainly not a life of prosperity. And, yet, these hardships happened to people of great faith, and the book of Hebrews says, "the world was not worthy of them" (v. 38). And so we see that sometimes, people of faith can experience great blessing, but at other times, they may experience suffering. Thankfully, regardless of what comes our way, we can be assured that nothing can separate us from the love of God, not even death (Romans 8:37–39).

What Is Faith?

Some people think there is some sort of automatic connection between faith and healing because they don't really understand what faith is. They seem to think faith is something we stir up in ourselves, like stirring up excitement. It is as if we can close our eyes tightly, clench our fists, and yell "Argh!" and our faith will get stronger.

If you are like many Christians, you have probably already thought of Hebrews 11:1: "Now faith is confidence in what we hope for and assurance about what we do not see." How helpful do you think this verse would be to explain what faith is to the average person who didn't grow up in church? If I say, "An apple is red," or, "An apple is round," or, "An apple is something that can fill you up," that isn't a definition of an apple as such. And while Hebrews 11:1 does describe faith when it says "faith is," it doesn't offer a definition of faith.

So what is Hebrews 11:1 saying? When the author tells us that faith is "assurance about what we do not see," the author does not mean, as someone might wrongly suppose, that faith is being certain of the existence of an invisible God. And having "confidence in what we hope for" does not mean that faith equals being sure that God is going to give you everything you ask for in prayer. Rather, later in the same chapter the author clarifies that the people in the faith hall of fame "were still living by faith when they died" because, although "they did not receive the things promised" in their lifetime (Hebrews 11:13), due to their faith they had *confidence in* and were *hoping* "for a better country—a heavenly one" (v. 16). So we might paraphrase Hebrews 11:1 as teaching that faith in God gives us certainty regarding what we hope for in the future, after death, because God has made promises to us. And the author of Hebrews illustrates this by teaching us about the heroes of faith who had deep trust, or reliance, on God, regardless of their sometimes horrific circumstances, and even though they hadn't yet received what God had promised.

Faith, then, is trust in God or believing in God. In fact, there is only one Greek word (*pistis*) used in the New Testament for "faith," "trust," or "belief." We aren't called to just "believe that" God exists, but rather to "believe in" God and to "believe in" Jesus (Acts 16:31). As an analogy, picture a modern-day action movie. Someone is perilously hanging from the edge of a cliff. The hero reaches out his muscular arm to pull the frightened person to safety. The hero says, "Take my hand." The other person replies, "I can't. I'm scared!" The hero says, "Do you believe in me?" The person hanging from the ledge says, "Yes." The hero responds, "Then take my hand." We understand that if the individual in danger actually has faith in the hero, they will commit themselves to the hero by taking the hero's hand. Then, of course, the hero pulls the person to safety—tragedy averted! Whew! Having faith in God is kind of like that.

Faith means believing in God by committing our whole self to God and God's ways. Faith is not, as some prosperity teachers suggest, "a spiritual force, a spiritual energy, a spiritual power." Faith does not, then, make "the laws of the spirit world function."[8] Rather, having faith simply means that you believe and trust in the Lord. It means you believe that God is able. You have faith that God cares for you. You trust God for your salvation. This is what faith is.

Faith ≠ Positive Confession

This means faith is not equal to positive confession. Some prosperity gospel teachers have claimed that you need to exercise your faith by confessing what you desire—only then will God give you what you wish for. This implies that our confession must always be positive. That is, they claim, "We as believers, as Christians, should never talk defeat. We should never talk failure. If you talk about your trials, your difficulties, your lack of faith, your lack of money—faith will shrivel and dry up."[9] The idea is that we should not engage in negative confession because we will end up inviting bad events into our lives. Such negative confession is, they wrongly suppose, the opposite of faith, whereas positive confession is how we express our faith. Therefore, some claim that "if you confess sickness, it will develop sickness within your system. If you talk about your doubts and fears, they will become stronger. If you confess the lack of finances, it will stop the money from coming in."[10] This is dangerous teaching. First, the concept of exercising your faith is not found in the Bible. More important, though, the Bible never teaches us to deny our present circumstances by pretending that negative things aren't happening in our lives.

Stop and think for a moment about the logic of positive confession teaching. It makes little sense. Positive confession leaves little to no room for lamenting, and there is a whole book in the Bible called Lamentations. One would feel trapped in a world of depression, sickness, and fear, because to talk about such experiences would open the door to those things. You could never really admit you are sick. You would be able to call someone to pray for you, but you couldn't tell them why to pray for you, because if you admitted that you were sick, that would be a negative confession, which would welcome sickness into your life. Yet Scripture never instructs us to deny our symptoms.

Many sincere Christians have wasted their time trying to "exercise their faith"—and this is not faith—by trying to convince themselves through positive confession that God has already healed them, even though they are still suffering from sickness. We don't manipulate God with our confession. Instead, we must humbly come to God, and like the man who had leprosy, kneel and acknowledge, "Lord, if you are willing, you can make me clean" (Matthew 8:2).

Faith ≠ Expectations

To further explain the meaning of faith, faith does not equal expectations. I have heard too many preachers claim that God won't work in your life if you don't *expect* God to.

Following this line of thinking, some claim, if you don't expect God to heal you, it won't happen. We need to be clear though. Our faith is in God, not in what God may or may not do, and not in whether or not God is going to heal someone. Our faith is in God—period. We believe in God—period. We trust in God—period—even when healing doesn't come. On the one hand, if I expect nothing from God, then I probably don't have faith in God. Given that God cares for us, I expect that God will provide for me and heal some people. Faith, however, comes first, then expectations. These are not the same thing. God asks us to have faith, not necessarily to expect. The result is that we can have great faith and trust in God, even when we have little to no expectations of God producing certain results. Again, faith doesn't equal expectations. It is too much to claim that *expectancy* "sets the stage for a miracle. . . . It influences Heaven. It starts things to happen."[11] On the other hand, we can affirm that our *faith* in God may set the stage for a miracle.

A few verses in the Bible might appear, on the face of it, to contradict what I'm saying. I think especially of Mark 11:23–24 and James 1:6–7. The passage from James reads, "But when you ask, you must believe and not doubt, because the one who doubts is like a wave of the sea. . . . That person should not expect to receive anything from the Lord." From these verses, it might seem that faith is the same as expectation. Furthermore, at first glance this passage almost makes it sound like if you have the right kind of faith, you will always get what you pray for.

When we continue to read through James, however, we learn that sometimes people do not receive what they pray for because they "ask with wrong motives" and are primarily concerned with their own "pleasures" (James 4:3). Plus, if we remember that faith means trusting in God and being committed to God, it is clear that when James said we "must believe" (1:6), he wasn't indicating that we must have expectant certainty. Rather, he meant that we must give our full loyalty to God. And when James said we must "not doubt," he wasn't saying we can't have any mental doubts that God might not do what we are asking for. Instead, he meant that our faith and commitment to God must not waver . . . "like a wave" (v. 6). In other words, the book of James calls us to have faith, which is total allegiance to God and trust in God, because God "gives [wisdom] generously" (1:5).[12]

The meaning of Mark 11:23–24 is similar to the meaning of the previous passage from James. In these verses, Jesus declared, "Truly I tell you, if anyone says to this mountain, 'Go, throw yourself into the sea,' and does not doubt in their heart but believes that what they say will happen, it will be done for them. Therefore I tell you, whatever you ask for in prayer, believe that you have received it, and it will be yours." This passage is not a universal and unconditional promise that we will always get what we pray for if we expect we will get it. Even proponents of prosperity teaching, such as Fred Price, recognize that when Jesus speaks of "whatever you ask for in prayer" (Mark 11:24), it doesn't mean that a woman can pray and "believe God for" or "claim" the husband of her choice, or that a man can realistically expect to "believe that I can eat as much of this cherry pie as I want and it is not going to make me fat" (these comical examples are real life stories Fred Price has encountered).[13]

Even faith, when rightly understood (as trust and commitment), doesn't guarantee the outcome we desire. We know this because Jesus added another aspect of effective prayer in the following verse: forgiveness (v. 25). In light of this, and the rest of the Bible's teaching on prayer, it is clear that in Mark 11:23–24, Jesus' primary concern is that he wants to encourage his disciples to "have faith in God" when they pray (v. 22). This passage, then, is not a guarantee that all mountains will be moved when we pray with expectation, but an appeal that we must have faith in God if we are going to see any mountains moved.[14] Similarly, when Jesus stated, "Ask and it will be given to you . . . For everyone who asks receives" (Matthew 7:7–8), he was not making a guarantee that God will give us everything we ask for; rather, these words are simply meant to encourage us to ask God for whatever we need, given that God will "give good gifts to those who ask him" (v. 11).

Faith Beyond Our Expectations

No story better illustrates the difference between faith and expectations than the resurrection of Lazarus in the gospel of John, chapter 11. As the story begins, Martha's brother Lazarus was sick. Martha sent for Jesus to come and heal Lazarus and because of her faith in Jesus, Martha expected Jesus was going to heal her brother (John 11:21). But, this isn't what happened. Instead, Jesus waited a few days and purposely didn't show up in Bethany, where Martha was, until Lazarus was already dead. If faith is the same thing as expectation, Martha's faith would have been shattered since her expectation didn't come to pass. Yet, in spite of this tragedy, Martha still maintained her faith in Jesus. When Jesus arrived, she told him, "I know that even now God will give you whatever you ask" (v. 22). Then out of her lips came the fullest confession of faith in the whole of the Gospel of John: "Yes, Lord," she told him, "I believe that you are the Messiah, the Son of God, who is to come into the world" (v. 27). Notice that these words didn't come from someone who had just witnessed a miracle, but from someone who was grieving the loss of her brother.

So Martha still had faith in Jesus, even though she wasn't expecting Jesus to raise her brother from the dead. And God worked in a way that was different from and beyond what she was expecting. Jesus told her that her brother would rise again, and Martha agreed that Lazarus would "rise again in the resurrection at the last day" (v. 24)—as in, "when everyone else rises." Jesus then told people to move the stone that was covering the entrance to the tomb where Lazarus was buried, but Martha objected: "By this time there is a bad odor, for he has been there four days" (v. 39). Again, she was not expecting Jesus to raise her brother from the dead. But that is precisely what Jesus did. Thank God that God is not limited by our expectations! While it is good and right for us to expect things from God, our faith is not in what we expect God to do. Our faith always has to be *in God*.

Faith is not a technique we use to manipulate God to heal us or give us anything else in life. When people think there is some sort of a faith recipe for healing—whether it's having enough faith, exercising their faith through positive confession, or expecting things from God—they have taken their eyes off of God and put them on themselves. They have put faith *in faith*, rather than putting their faith *in God*, and turned God into a cosmic bellhop who is required to do whatever we ask if only we will use the right faith technique. Again, faith is simply our belief in and trust in God.

How Much Faith?

Even after we recognize the true meaning of faith, the question might linger: How much faith is required before God will heal someone? People can have different levels of faith. Remember that faith also means "trust," and some people do trust God more than others. And so, "the apostles said to the Lord, 'Increase our faith!'" (Luke 17:5). It is wrong, however, to think God only responds to people who have *lots* of faith or, perhaps, people who have victorious faith, whatever that means. It would seem strange to think that anyone with faith can be saved by Jesus Christ, but that for someone to receive an answer to prayer—for example, for healing—they need to have a whole lot of faith. Is God gracious only in salvation? No, God is always gracious. And God heals people out of compassion and grace, not because people deserve healing due to their levels of faith.

The Bible only records two instances when Jesus commended people for their "great faith." In one story, a Roman centurion asked Jesus to heal his paralyzed servant, who was "suffering terribly" (Matthew 8:6). Jesus asked if he should go to heal him, but the Roman replied, "Lord, I do not deserve to have you come under my roof. But just say the word, and my servant will be healed. For I myself am a man under authority, with soldiers under me. I tell this one, 'Go,' and he goes; and that one, 'Come,' and he comes. I say to my servant, 'Do this,' and he does it" (vv. 8–9). Jesus was amazed at the centurion's response and praised his great faith.

The other instance involves a Canaanite woman who approached Jesus on behalf of her daughter, who was "demon-possessed and suffering terribly" (Matthew 15:22). Jesus probed the woman's faith, testing her to see if she (and those around her) recognized the universal love of God, and the woman did not relent in her request. As a result, Jesus assured her, "you have great faith" (v. 28). In both of these stories, Jesus did *not* say that he decided to heal the person *because of* the amount of faith they had. Rather, he simply observed their great faith. Why did he do this? Biblical scholars agree that the reason Jesus highlighted the faith of these two people is that Jesus was commending these non-Jewish people—a Roman centurion and a Canaanite woman—in order to encourage his Jewish audience to have the same faith in him that these Gentiles had, and to challenge the common Jewish belief that God's grace did not extend to the Gentiles. That's why Jesus said to the Roman centurion, "I have not found anyone *in Israel* with such great faith" (Matthew 8:10).[15]

Little Faith

As with great faith, Jesus did not speak often of a person having "little faith," and when he did, it was never in connection to healing. Once, Jesus said that those who don't trust God to provide for their basic needs have little faith, given that "God clothes the grass of the field, which is here today and tomorrow is thrown into the fire" (Matthew

6:30). On another occasion, Jesus observed the disciples' little faith when they were afraid their boat was going to sink during a "furious storm" (Matthew 8:24–26). And many sermons have been preached on the story of Peter walking on water. He began to sink, and Jesus then remarked on his "little faith" (Matthew 14:31). Finally, Jesus mentioned the little faith of the disciples when they were concerned about their lack of bread, even though Jesus had already miraculously provided bread on more than one occasion (Matthew 16:8–10).

Sometimes I can identify with the people in these stories and their "little faith." But these stories about little faith aren't discouraging. On the contrary, we see through the people in the stories that Jesus worked miracles despite their little faith. Just as God is not limited by our expectations, God is not limited by our level of faith. And so, Jesus saved the disciples and calmed the stormy sea, even though they had little faith. And Peter may have begun to sink, but he still walked on water. I seem to remember Jesus saying something about having "faith as small as a mustard seed" (Matthew 17:20).

When Jesus spoke of faith and healing, he rarely mentioned how *much* faith people had. Instead, Jesus just spoke generally about "your faith" (Mark 10:52). At the same time, it does seem that unbelief can hinder miracles. When Jesus was teaching in the synagogue in his hometown, many people "took offense at him," and the Bible tells us that, as a result, Jesus "did not do many miracles there because of their lack of faith [or, more accurately in some Bible translations, their unbelief]" (Matthew 13:57–58). The people in Jesus' hometown didn't believe in him because they didn't understand who he was. Nevertheless, Jesus still "laid his hands on a few sick people and healed them" (Mark 6:5 ESV). And I am reminded once again that God is not limited by the amount of faith I have, or by the faith of anyone else for that matter.

The teaching that we need lots of faith to be healed has ironically led to fewer healings because it can make people too scared to pray for healing since they fear they don't have great faith. Rather than giving up on prayer, whenever you feel like your faith is small, you can cry out to God, "I believe; help my unbelief" (Mark 9:24 ESV).

Healing or No Healing

You may be left wondering, what then shall I do? Or, how should I pray for healing? If you think you must use a specific technique or formula when praying for healing, you may have a hangover from prosperity teaching. We cannot manipulate God into being gracious toward us—grace is a gift, and that means we don't create it and we don't earn it. We should pray for healing, and we should do so with faith in God. After all, God "is able to do immeasurably more than all we ask or imagine" (Ephesians 3:20). And so we should pray. But we should also remember that there is no *right way* to pray. History shows us that God has responded to all kinds of different people with different ways of praying for healing. Some praying for others to be healed touched them, at times anointing them with oil. Others merely spoke. Some prayed loudly, while others were quiet and calm. Some prayed for an extended period of time, while others saw healing instantly. Some received a revelation from God about a coming healing, and others just prayed with hope. Some were in a church service, some were not. And some had peculiar teaching, while others didn't.[16]

So what about Jim who looked into his mirror, confessed his healing, and was healed and released from the hospital? In light of all I find in the Bible, I am convinced that God did heal Jim. But I am also convinced that it was not because of how Jim acted. It was not because of Jim at all. Instead, God, in grace, responded to Jim's faith. The story might not have ended as it did, though. Many people with great faith, even those who have "claimed their healing," have continued to suffer through their pain. And many have died in the midst of having great faith.

Sometimes we are too prone to look for God only in the victory of Christ's resurrection, and by analogy in the victory of our present healings. We need to remember, however, that God was also present in the suffering of the cross of Christ, and by analogy in our present sufferings. In the midst of suffering, we can affirm with Paul that God's "grace is sufficient" (2 Corinthians 12:9). And just as we pray (and should pray) for God to heal people through the power of the Holy Spirit, we can also pray for God's grace to endure suffering. Blessed be the name of the Lord!

Father, forgive us if we have ever made anyone feel guilty about not having enough faith. And help us forgive others who may have caused us to feel this way. At the same time, increase our faith. Help us trust in you and to pray for healing for ourselves or for others. Help us "understand the incredible greatness of God's power for us who believe" (Ephesians 1:19–20). Give us the compassion of Christ. And for those who are not healed, provide the strength to endure as we await the redemption of our bodies at the resurrection.

Questions for Reflection or Discussion

1. What does it mean to have faith?
2. Can you identify any ways your understanding of healing might have been shaped by prosperity teaching?
3. Have you ever heard someone tell another person they don't have enough faith for God to do something in their life?

4. Why do you suppose God sometimes responds to a person's faith by granting their prayer request, whereas other times God doesn't give that same person what they desire?

5. How likely are you to pray for someone to be healed?

CHAPTER 6

MEASURING UP?

Spiritual Gifts

MEASURING UP?

When I was studying in seminary, I sometimes got overwhelmed and discouraged. I can still hear myself: *I can't do it. I'm never going to finish this. I can't see the light at the end of the tunnel. This is too much for me.* Instead of remaining in the depths of despair, I occasionally went out for lunch with a particular friend of mine. This fellowship always gave me the pick-me-up I needed. Aside from the fact that I enjoy good food, my friend was great at encouraging me. I never had to tell him how I was feeling—it just seemed to come naturally to him. I can still hear him now: "You can do it, Andrew! Boy, I wish I was as smart as you. You're making great progress." I would walk away from the restaurant with a spring in my step and a smile on my face, feeling like I could conquer the world. If it wasn't for friends like him, I probably wouldn't be where I am today. My friend has the spiritual gift of encouragement.

So Many Gifts!

Encouragement? Yes, that is a spiritual gift (Romans 12:8). Sometimes people think of spiritual gifts only as things that are dramatic and spectacular, but there is more to spiritual gifts than miracles. Certainly things like healing can be gifts of the Spirit, but the New Testament describes many different spiritual gifts (Romans 12:6–8; 1 Corinthians 12:8–10, 27–28; 1 Peter 4:8–11; and perhaps Ephesians 4:7–11). Giving is also a spiritual gift—anyone can give (and all the pastors said, "Amen"), but the Spirit enables some people to thrive when they are giving. I see the gift of serving present in people who regularly and cheerfully stay behind after a church event to stack chairs and mop the floor. I see people using the gifts of helping, mercy, administration, leadership, and hospitality at the community center my church has started. None of these gifts sound all that supernatural. In fact, they sound quite normal. But these spiritual gifts are all supernatural in the sense that the Spirit is involved. The Bible affirms, "All these are the work of one and the same Spirit" (1 Corinthians 12:11).

Sometimes people aren't aware of the gifts the Spirit has given them. After all, when people have the gift of administration, or any other less dramatic gift, they don't start shaking, talking funny, and speaking like the King James Version of the Bible—"thus saith the Lord." Instead, they just serve with excellence as enabled by the Spirit. I hope this will be encouraging to some of you who thought you had no spiritual gift just because you don't have a more noticeable gift, like prophecy or speaking in tongues. Perhaps you thought you didn't measure up to those whose gifts were more dramatic. We don't all have the same gifts, and that is the way it is supposed to be. The Scripture says, "We have different gifts, according to the grace given to each of us" (Romans 12:6).

You can find a lot of spiritual gifts in the New Testament (see the following table). There could be even more. Some people from church history have claimed to have the gift of prayer, tears, and visions.[1] It is evident from looking at the lists in the Bible that none of the biblical authors intended to provide a list outlining what all the spiritual gifts are. For example, teaching and prophecy appear in three of the passages, whereas encouragement only shows up in Romans 12, and healing only in 1 Corinthians 12. Instead of providing an exhaustive list of spiritual gifts, the biblical authors simply explained some of the many ways the Holy Spirit works through people.

There's No Such Thing as Spiritual Gifts (Kind of)

Actually, for all that I've said about spiritual gifts, there really is no such thing as "spiritual gifts" . . . kind of. Go ahead. Search your Bible. You won't find the phrase "spiritual gift" anywhere. You found it in 1 Corinthians 12 and 14? Well, it isn't actually in the original Greek language in which the New Testament was first written. Let me explain.[2]

Spiritual Gifts Listed in the New Testament			
ROMANS 12:6–8	1 CORINTHIANS 12:8–10, 27–28	EPHESIANS 4:7–11	1 PETER 4:8–11
Prophesying	Message of wisdom	Apostles	Hospitality
Serving	Message of knowledge	Prophets	Serving
Teaching	Faith	Evangelists	Speaking
Encouraging	Healings	Pastors	
Giving	Miracles	Teachers	
Leadership	Prophecy		
Showing mercy	Distinguishing between spirits		
	Tongues		
	Interpretation of tongues		
	Apostles		
	Prophets		
	Teachers		
	Helping others		
	Administration		

Most English translations of the Bible present Paul writing about "spiritual gifts" in 1 Corinthians 12:1 and 14:1. In English, these verses read:

Now concerning spiritual gifts, brothers, I do not want you to be uninformed. (1 Corinthians 12:1 ESV)

Follow the way of love and eagerly desire gifts of the Spirit, especially prophecy. (1 Corinthians 14:1)

The word *gifts*, however, doesn't actually occur in these verses in Greek. The Greek word Paul did use in these verses is *pneumatika*, literally meaning "spirituals" or things having to do with the Spirit. *Spirituals* is not a technical term Paul used in reference to a limited number of ways the Spirit works, that is, "spiritual gifts." Rather, in the Bible the word *spiritual* is used in a number of contexts to describe the general presence and work of the Holy Spirit. So, for example, the church is a "spiritual house" (1 Peter 2:5).

Another key Greek word Paul used when he talked about things like the gifts of teaching, healing, tongues, and so forth, is *charismata*, for example, in 1 Corinthians 12:4 and 31. This word literally means "gifts." Again, this is not a technical term Paul used only to refer to a special way the Spirit works, that is, "spiritual gifts"; Paul used this word in multiple ways. For example, he described salvation as a "gift" (Romans 6:23).

Paul did not create a special category limiting the number of spiritual gifts. Rather, when Paul talked about "spirituals" or "gifts," he was simply describing *some* of the ways the Spirit uses people and enables people to minister. The Spirit can use believers in many other ways. Many Christians, however, reserve the term "spiritual gifts" to refer to the list of gifts I have included in the table above. That is, they imagine a special kind of box filled with spiritual gifts and say that only those gifts that appear in these New Testament lists belong in this special box. The result is that even though the Spirit empowers my friend's talent in artistic designs, as in Exodus 35:31–32, and even though this is a tremendous blessing to her church community, this artistic ability doesn't get counted as a spiritual gift because it isn't in the spiritual gifts box. Paul, however, didn't have a special category that limits the spiritual gifts. As I said, he never used the phrase "spiritual gifts."

But does the Spirit give us gifts? Yes, by all means— the gifts Paul described in his letters are, again, "the work of one and the same Spirit" (1 Corinthians 12:11). But we should not limit what we consider to be a spiritual gift to those listed in the table I've included above. These are some of the ways the Spirit can be at work among us, but not all. So, rather than only asking, "What are your spiritual gifts?" you might also ask, "What are the ways the Spirit uses you?"

Problem Gifts?

Among the gifts of the Spirit listed in the New Testament, tongues and the interpretation of tongues are probably the strangest of the bunch (1 Corinthians 14:27–28). Even though you can find many instances of Christians speaking in tongues throughout the long history of the church and demonstrating many other "strange" gifts of the Spirit, too, speaking in tongues grew in practice with the development of the Pentecostal-Charismatic movement in the twentieth century.[3] And with growth in practice, came growth in confusion and abuse.

I remember one Sunday things didn't go so well at church. That morning two people decided to start giving a message in tongues—at the same time. This clearly went against Paul's teaching that believers should share a message "one at a time" (1 Corinthians 14:27), so it left everyone in the service feeling awkward. The pastor tried to be gentle in his response. From behind the pulpit he said, "Amen" and "Praise the Lord" loudly a number of times into the microphone. His attempt to drown them out and hopefully get at least one person to stop didn't work. I guess both people felt the Spirit needed them each to speak at that moment. As a result, the pastor ended up asking them both to stop.

That's not a particularly encouraging story. And if you already felt uneasy about the gift of tongues, the story likely doesn't make you feel any better about it. Nevertheless, just because people might use this gift, or any gift, inappropriately, doesn't mean we should neglect it. Just because a gift is misused doesn't mean it is bad. It can still have great potential if used properly. We are the problem, not the gift. We must heed the Scripture's warning: "Do not put out the Spirit's fire. . . . Hold on to the good" (1 Thessalonians 5:19–21). Therefore, we should "not forbid speaking in tongues" (1 Corinthians 14:39). Although I have the opportunity to worship in different churches on occasion,

I haven't heard a message in tongues for quite some time. This saddens me because I think many churches are missing out on one of the ways the Spirit wants to speak in the church.

In the Bible, the word *tongue* most often simply means "language." When people engage in the gift of "speaking in different kinds of tongues" (1 Corinthians 12:10), they might speak in human or angelic tongues (1 Corinthians 13:1). The gift of tongues by itself isn't helpful for those listening, though, since "no one understands" those speaking in tongues as "they utter mysteries by the Spirit" (1 Corinthians 14:2). Therefore, in contrast to tongues as a language of prayer (see chapter 4 in this book), when a message in tongues is offered to the church, Paul instructed that "someone must interpret" (1 Corinthians 14:27). The result isn't a translation as such, but the interpretation does communicate the overall message for the benefit of the congregation in a language they can understand.

I used to think if someone interpreted their own message in tongues, they must have been faking it or they were too scared to wait to see if someone else would interpret. I eventually learned, however, that although the interpretation often comes from someone else (1 Corinthians 14:28), the interpretation might also come from the person who gave the message in tongues, for Paul said, "The one who speaks in a tongue should pray that they may interpret what they say" (v. 13).

Unclear Gifts

While many of the gifts of the Spirit are easy to identify, like healing or serving, it isn't completely clear how some other gifts listed in the New Testament function. This is particularly true of the gifts of distinguishing between spirits and the messages of wisdom and knowledge. To be sure, many pastors have preached sermons and many people have written books that explain with great certainty what these gifts are. The apostle Paul, however, never actually explained what he meant by these gifts. When people teach about these gifts of the Spirit, therefore, they usually describe— probably legitimate—experiences of the Spirit they have witnessed and then label those experiences with the terms that Paul used in the Bible. But the experiences they describe and the experiences Paul described in the Bible aren't necessarily one and the same.

What is the gift of discerning or "distinguishing between spirits" (1 Corinthians 12:10)? Again, Scripture doesn't explicitly tell us. Some people think it is the Spirit-given ability to tell if someone is acting from their own human spirit, or as influenced by the Holy Spirit or, alternatively, by a demonic spirit. Others suppose that this gift refers to the ability to interpret the source and significance of prophecy, given that Paul mentioned the gift of discernment immediately after the gift of prophecy (1 Corinthians 12:10).

The precise meaning of a word or "message of wisdom"

and a word or "message of knowledge" (1 Corinthians 12:8) is also unclear. Although some teachers try to make clear distinctions between these two gifts, in my experience most Christians understandably don't try to distinguish between these gifts. Of course, it's quite possible there is no hard and fast distinction between these gifts, much like the gifts of healing and miracles are not mutually exclusive. Professor Anthony Thiselton observed that among New Testament scholars "there is no consensus whatever about any clear distinction between" the two.[4] Likewise, in one church where I pastored, if someone presented a spontaneous message in English to the church, we would just say that someone "gave *a word* in church today."

Many people think of the messages of wisdom and knowledge as spontaneous—even miraculous—messages revealed from God. That is, some people suppose that it must involve knowledge that the person could not have known without revelatory insight from the Spirit. I can understand how someone would make this conclusion; in my own life, at times someone has prayed for me in a way that was exactly what I needed even though I hadn't shared my struggles with the person praying for me.

I'm not convinced, though, that messages of wisdom and knowledge are always spontaneous and dramatic. And in contrast to those with a dramatic conception of messages of wisdom and knowledge, some people think these gifts refer to any time that the Spirit helps us clarify Scripture for others or apply truth to a particular situation in a nonspectacular way. Others think the gift of wisdom, specifically, could simply be preaching about Christ, who is "the wisdom of God" (1 Corinthians 1:24). You might say, "This can't be what these gifts refer to. They have to be dramatic revelations from God—they are *spiritual* gifts." But as I have already emphasized, spiritual gifts aren't always dramatic. They can be natural abilities enhanced by the Spirit.

Which Gift?

Sometimes it won't be clear which spiritual gift is at play. Peter, seemingly without prior knowledge, asked Ananias, "How is it that Satan has so filled your heart that you have lied to the Holy Spirit and have kept for yourself some of the money you received for the land?" (Acts 5:3). This could be an example of a word of knowledge. But it could also be an example of distinguishing between spirits, or even prophecy. While I affirm that the Spirit inspired Peter at this moment, the book of Acts doesn't tell us which gift of the Spirit was at work. Nevertheless, we shouldn't just throw up our hands and say, "I have no idea how the Spirit works or what spiritual gifts are!" Even if we don't have clarity in how to label the gift being used, we do know the Spirit is at work. When we study the variety of ways the Spirit gifts people (see the table on page 128), we see that the Spirit brings about different kinds of miracles and enables people to speak and serve in a variety of ways.

What About Prophecy?

As with other gifts, Christians have different views regarding what constitutes prophecy. But unlike the gifts I've already discussed, the Bible actually says quite a lot to help us understand what prophecy really is. Many people in Pentecostal-Charismatic circles define prophecy too narrowly. When they say someone "prophesied over" them (I'm not sure why it is always "over" and not "to," or "under"), they usually mean that someone told them something about their future.

While prophecy might refer to the future (Acts 21:10–11), it can refer to much more. In fact, when prophecy is mentioned in Romans and 1 Corinthians, Paul doesn't mention any predictive element. Furthermore, when we look at the content of prophecy in the Old Testament, we find that prophecies were generally more concerned with contemporary events than with the future. Their message was usually something like, "Turn from your evil ways and your evil practices" (Zechariah 1:4). Prophecy, then, can also occur when someone speaks up when they see a problem of sin. Moreover, Paul added that prophecy takes place when "the one who prophesies speaks to people for their strengthening, encouraging and comfort" (1 Corinthians 14:3).

I once had a student sitting in my office, slouched over on a chair. He was feeling worthless and insecure about his abilities as a student, though I could see he was doing good work. I could tell by the marks on his arms that his depression had plagued him previously in life. As I spoke with him I encouraged him and reminded him of his identity as a child of God and as someone who is made in the image of God. I did not shake or speak in a strange voice, which many people seem to think is a necessary marker of prophecy. And I never told the student I was prophesying. Yet when the student left, I was certain God had used me to prophesy to him. I had a sense of the Spirit's presence, and I knew the words I shared were not something I had come up with on my own.

Some people suggest that prophecy is nothing more than the preaching of the Word of God. While I affirm that prophecy might take place as someone preaches, my previous story illustrates that prophecy isn't limited to a church service, just like the gift of healing and other gifts aren't limited to church services. Furthermore, Paul's description of prophecy indicates that prophecy isn't only the result of a pastor studying and preparing a sermon, but it can include some sense of spontaneity, for Paul spoke of prophecy happening after "a revelation comes to someone" from God (1 Corinthians 14:30).

Of course, if someone does claim to prophesy, it doesn't mean we should just accept what they have to say as coming directly from God. When prophecy occurs, we "should weigh carefully what is said" (1 Corinthians 14:29). We should consider who is giving the prophecy as well. This includes taking into account the doctrine or theology of the prophet (1 John 4:1–3). Yet, if someone performs miracles or has the gift of healing, many people are prone to listen to *anything* that person says. Remember, someone who has the gift of healing doesn't necessarily have the gift of teaching. We also need to remember Jesus' warning that there are "false prophets" who can even drive out demons and perform other miracles (Matthew 7:15–23). Rather than look for miracles when evaluating prophecy, or truth in general for that matter, Jesus said we should take into account the person's fruit. The early church followed Jesus' teaching by watching for hypocrisy and observing a prophet's behavior—were they meek, gentle, and humble like Jesus?—and their desire for money—would they prophesy if they weren't paid?[5] This would be wise advice for us today too.

Right Gift, Wrong Attitude

It seems when people teach on the spiritual gifts today, the focus is usually on explaining what the gifts are. When the apostle Paul wrote to churches about the spiritual gifts, however, he was not concerned with explaining what the gifts were—they probably already knew that since they did "not lack any spiritual gift" (1 Corinthians 1:7). And yet, Paul wrote, "Now about the gifts of the Spirit, brothers and sisters, I do not want you to be uninformed" (1 Corinthians 12:1). Many people today remain uninformed about the value of each and every spiritual gift.

People can say they think all the gifts are important, but their hearts often betray them. They might think, *Serving is good, but, boy oh boy, I'd sure like to heal someone!* Or, *I want to be a prophet, or to give a word of knowledge. But, helping? Meh* . . . And let's be honest, having the gift of healing or miracles can get you your own TV show, but probably not the gift of encouragement, unless, perhaps, you are Joel Osteen. I imagine when you started reading this chapter some of you likely said, "Okay, I know there are all kinds of spiritual gifts, but let's get to the *good* ones!" Such thoughts indicate that we don't value all the gifts equally.

Many teachers list the spiritual gifts in categories such as gifts of revelation, utterance, and power. I've also seen other groupings like gifts of leadership, signs, and service; or manifestation, motivational, and ministry gifts. By contrast, when the biblical authors described the spiritual gifts, they didn't categorize them. Instead, they just listed the gifts all together. Unlike us, the Bible doesn't distinguish between the dramatic gifts and the less spectacular gifts. Instead, Paul listed prophecy right beside service (Romans 12:6–7), and he sandwiched the gifts of helping and administration right between the gifts of healing and tongues (1 Corinthians 12:28). This is because all the gifts are important.

All the gifts are of value because they all have the same source. Paul emphasized this repeatedly: "There are different kinds of gifts, but *the same Spirit* distributes them. There are different kinds of service, but *the same Lord*. There are different kinds of working, but in all of them and in everyone it is *the same God* at work" (1 Corinthians 12:4–6). He continued by emphasizing how the message of wisdom and knowledge are by "the same Spirit" and that the gift of faith comes "by the same Spirit" and healing "by that one Spirit" (vv. 8–9). In case it wasn't clear, to conclude he stated one more time, "All these are the work of one and the same Spirit" (v. 11). *Same, same, same.* They are all *spiritual* gifts because they all have *the same* source, namely, the Holy Spirit. Therefore, when someone gives a message in tongues or a prophetic word in a church service, we should not think, *The Holy Spirit is finally at work here!* The reality is that the Spirit has already likely been at work as people used their gift of hospitality when they greeted people at the front door or as people engaged their gift of giving as the offering plate passed by. We need to recognize and value all the ways the gifts are present among us.

A Healthy Body

We need *all* the gifts of the Spirit to be present in our churches for the body of Christ to experience its greatest health. The only time you find the "body of Christ" analogy actually explained in the Bible is in connection with the spiritual gifts in Romans 12 and 1 Corinthians 12. Basically, Paul described how each person with a different gift from the Spirit contributes to the church similarly to the way different body parts are important for a human body to function well. He asked, "If the whole body were an eye, where would the sense of hearing be? If the whole body were an ear, where would the sense of smell be? . . . If they were all one part, where would the body be?" (1 Corinthians 12:17, 19). If a church were full of people gifted in only prophecy or teaching, it would be big on truth, but people in need might not find much help. Similarly, if the church were full of people only gifted in mercy, the church would seem caring, but it might lack direction. We need the different body parts, or spiritual gifts, because they are all important to the well-being of the church.

I need my ears to hear the doorbell when the pizza delivery person comes. I have my feet to walk me to the door. My hands help me take the pizza inside my house. And I need my mouth (praise the Lord!) to eat the pizza. Without each of these body parts, I might still be able to get my pizza, but it would be more of a challenge. Likewise, without each of the gifts of the Spirit, the church may remain malnourished.

We need all types of gifted people in the church. "The eye cannot say to the hand, 'I don't need you!' And the head cannot say to the feet, 'I don't need you!'" (1 Corinthians 12:21). Likewise, those with the gift of prophecy should never say to those with the gift of hospitality, "I don't need you." Nor should those with the gift of serving say to those with the gift of tongues, "I don't need you." All the gifts are important.

Not for You

This all points to the fact that the gifts of the Spirit aren't primarily for our own personal benefit. God doesn't give us gifts so we can have some sort of a spiritual experience, an emotional high, or to build an international ministry with our name on it. The gifts are for the health of the church. They are for others. And we don't earn them. The gifts are not badges of honor or indicators of a higher level of spirituality. If they were, the Corinthian church would not have been so familiar with the spiritual gifts. This was a church with sexual immorality, disunity, and people getting drunk at communion (1 Corinthians 6 and 11). That's why the gifts are called spiritual *gifts*, not rewards. And we receive them by God's grace. In fact, the Greek word for *grace* (*charis*) is the foundation of the word *gifts* (*charismata*), and "we have different gifts [*charismata*], according to the grace [*charis*] given us" (Romans 12:6). God is gracious to us in giving us gifts so we can serve others. The Bible consistently reminds us that God gives them "for the common good" (1 Corinthians 12:7), "for the strengthening of the church" (1 Corinthians 14:26), and "to serve others, as faithful stewards of God's grace in its various forms" (1 Peter 4:10). Let us build up the church in love, using the gifts God has given each of us. My gift is for your well-being. And your gift may be for my well-being.

Getting Gifts

While this is all good, some of you have probably wondered where or how you can get the gifts of the Spirit. After all, you can't just order them on Amazon. Unfortunately, I don't see any formula or instruction manual in the Bible for how to get the spiritual gifts. The only advice I see in Scripture is that we should "eagerly desire gifts of the Spirit" (1 Corinthians 14:1). (This is certainly different from one common refrain, "seek not, forbid not.") I would add that we can ask God, who is generous. I've heard some preachers caution that we should "seek the Giver and not the gifts." And there is the danger of seeking the gifts for selfish reasons. Nevertheless, Jesus said, "If you, then, though you are evil, know how to give good gifts to your children, how much more will your Father in heaven give good gifts to those who ask him!" (Matthew 7:11).

Aside from simply asking God yourself, it is also possible that you might have a spiritual gift imparted to you through another person. Paul spoke of his desire to "impart . . . some spiritual gift" to Christians in Rome (Romans 1:11–12), and he implored Timothy, "Do not neglect your gift, which was given you through prophecy when the body of elders laid their hands on you" (1 Timothy 4:14). In these passages, it isn't quite clear whether Paul had spiritual gifts in mind. Regardless, the idea of "impartation" might sound kind of spooky, like some form of Christian magic. Nevertheless, if we can ask God to give us a gift, then surely it is okay for someone else to lay hands on us and pray for God to give us a gift, just as one might do when praying for someone to be healed. But crucially, whether it is you or someone else praying, the gift still remains a gift *of the Spirit*. No one who prays can control the Spirit.

Desiring and praying for spiritual gifts doesn't mean we should be choosy. Paul did say we should "desire the greater gifts" (1 Corinthians 12:31) and that we should especially pursue the gift of prophecy (1 Corinthians 14:1), but all he meant by this is that we should especially seek gifts that will benefit others in the church. That's why he went on to explain that "the one who prophesies is greater" than anyone who speaks in tongues because the one who prophesies "speaks to people for their strengthening, encouraging and comfort," whereas "no one understands" the person who speaks in tongues, unless someone interprets (vv. 5, 3, 2).[6] Overall, though, the Bible makes clear that we should be willing to serve in whatever way God wishes, whether that is through a more public gift, or a gift that doesn't attract attention. We don't get to determine which gift(s) we receive. Instead, the Spirit "distributes them . . . just as he determines" (1 Corinthians 12:11).

How will you know when you have received a gift from the Spirit? You might not. You might sense a prompting from God to minister in a particular way, like giving a message in tongues, or you might not feel or sense anything at all. For example, while others have observed the gift of teaching present in my life, I can't say I noticed any particular moment when I felt I received the gift.

All Gifted

Although we are told to desire the spiritual gifts, if you are a believer, you have the Spirit dwelling in you, and you have at least one gift of the Spirit. The Bible says that God gives gifts "to each one" for the common good (1 Corinthians

12:7), that the Spirit "gives them to each one" (v. 11), and that "God has arranged the parts in the body, *every one of them*, just as he wanted them to be" (v. 18). We are *all* parts of the body, and we are all gifted by the Spirit in some way, though we aren't always aware of it.

One way to figure out which gift(s) you have is by doing an online spiritual gifts assessment or inventory.[7] Such assessments serve as good reminders that the Spirit empowers all believers for ministry, not just professional clergy. They can also call attention to the diverse ways people can serve, and they encourage people to seriously consider what types of ministry they are best suited for. At the same time, these assessments are usually based only on a limited number of gifts listed in the New Testament, and, as I noted above, the Spirit might use you in more ways than those listed in the New Testament.[8]

Another (perhaps better) way to determine your spiritual gifts, although it doesn't produce the immediate results that spiritual gifts assessments provide, is to simply begin to serve in different ways and ask others what they observe. You should also ask yourself, "What am I good at? What am I passionate about?" Your answers likely indicate where the Spirit is at work in your life. Figuring out the name or title of the gift you have is not all that important. Rather, you should just aim to allow the Spirit to use you to serve others and build up the church.

Serve!

You have a spiritual gift, so serve! You are an important part of the body of Christ, and we need you—this is one reason Christians should stay in community with one another. When functioning correctly, the church is not "one big mouth and a lot of little ears," that is, the preacher and the congregation.[9] As the Scripture implores, "Each of you should use whatever gift you have received to serve others, as faithful stewards of God's grace in its various forms . . . so that in all things God may be praised through Jesus Christ. To him be the glory and the power for ever and ever. Amen" (1 Peter 4:10–11).

Father, thank you for the many ways you work among us by the Spirit. Help us recognize and value these ways. Forgive us for any pride we have had regarding the gifts of the Spirit. Please give us a desire for the gifts of the Spirit, and grant us hearts to serve in whatever way you determine is best.

Questions for Reflection or Discussion

1. What does it mean to have a spiritual gift?
2. Do you truly feel that all the spiritual gifts are important for the health of the church?

3. In what ways have you seen spiritual gifts at work in people from your church?
4. To what extent are you using your spiritual gifts to serve others?
5. Do you "eagerly desire the gifts of the Spirit" (1 Corinthians 14:1)? Are there any gifts of the Spirit you are not open to receiving?

CHAPTER 7

WHAT DOES IT MEAN TO BE SPIRIT-FILLED?

I magine. You pull the door open a crack and peer into the church sanctuary. Near the back of the room, a young woman stands with her hands raised high and her eyes shut tight, singing with much enthusiasm. Closer to the front, an older lady sits in her seat singing quietly with her head bowed and her hands folded in a position of prayer. Who is more spiritual—more Spirit-filled? Or perhaps the truly spiritual person is the young man playing guitar and leading worship from the stage. No, probably not. Surely one of these two ladies is the picture of spirituality. After all, who would really think of a *man* as spiritual, unless it was, perhaps, the pastor?

Spiritual = Strange?

After all I have said in this book, it is time to ask the question, what does it mean to be spiritual? In popular culture, this usually indicates some sort of mystical experience or spooky encounter. If you meditate regularly, believe in ghosts, or feel you have an unusual connection to nature, you might be considered spiritual. It also seems to help if you like crystals and butterflies. Even within the church, many people think that the word *spiritual* must indicate something or someone a little strange. Depending on how much exposure people have had to the Pentecostal-Charismatic movement, they might associate the word spiritual with people who claim to be inspired by the Spirit to bark like dogs, scream, or roll around on the floor. Such people exist—I've seen them! Whether inside the church or outside the church, it seems that *spiritual* sometimes just means "strange."

Some people try to justify their conclusion that it is spiritual to act strange by pointing to the eccentric behavior of prophets in the Old Testament. For example, Isaiah walked around naked (Isaiah 20:1–4)—some scholars say, wearing only an undergarment—and Ezekiel lay on his side for 430 days (Ezekiel 4:4–6). Some also point to Saul, who "changed into a different person" when the Spirit of the Lord came upon him and he prophesied (1 Samuel 10:6, 10). These examples, however, don't prove that one should expect to act strangely if one is to be truly spiritual. First of all, Saul might have just "changed into a different person" in the sense that "God changed Saul's heart" before he prophesied (v. 9). Furthermore, when you read about the prophets in the Old Testament, you don't get the sense that the prophets were *usually* ecstatic and acting strangely. To illustrate the point, when Elijah had his standoff at Mount Carmel, it was the prophets of Baal who "danced around the altar they had made," shouted, slashed themselves with swords, and engaged in "frantic prophesying," while they endeavored to get Baal to send fire on their sacrifice (1 Kings 18:26–29). By contrast, when Elijah called on God to send fire on his sacrifice, he merely "stepped forward and prayed" (v. 36). Strange or out-of-the-ordinary things might happen when people experience the Spirit—like speaking in tongues, dreams, or visions (Joel 2:28)—but such experiences are not the primary indicator of spirituality.

Biblical Spirituality

In the Bible, the word *spiritual* isn't a generic word used to refer to the nonphysical world or to a "religious" person. Rather, *spiritual* means specifically something that is related to the work of the Holy Spirit.[1] For example, the Bible refers to people who make up the church as "a spiritual house" (1 Peter 2:5) since the Spirit dwells in the church (1 Corinthians 3:16), salvation is a "spiritual blessing" (Romans 15:27) because a person is born again by the Holy Spirit (John 3:6–8), and one can sing "spiritual songs" as they are "filled with the Spirit" (Ephesians 5:18–19 ESV). Again, spiritual simply means having to do with the work of the Holy Spirit.

This definition of *spiritual* implies that to be Spirit-filled is not the same as being emotional. Certainly, the Spirit may be experienced in a way that stirs the emotions and leads a person to exclaim, "God is really among you!" (1 Corinthians 14:25). Nevertheless, when the Bible mentions experiencing the Spirit, it rarely discusses what the experience was like or the emotions it might have aroused. Instead, the focus is placed on the life-changing results of the experience.

Biblical spirituality refers first and foremost to the ways in which the Spirit shapes us to become more like Jesus Christ. After the Spirit descended upon Jesus at his baptism, Jesus was "full of the Holy Spirit" (Luke 4:1), even "without limit" (John 3:34). As a result, Jesus cast out demons "by the Spirit of God" (Matthew 12:28), and he engaged in all kinds of ministry "in the power of the Spirit" (Luke 4:14). All Jesus was and did when he walked on earth, then, indicates what it means to be spiritual.

Character

One of the first things that comes to mind when Christians think about Jesus is his morally perfect character. When Jesus overcame the Devil's temptation, he entered the wilderness "full of the Holy Spirit" (Luke 4:1), and forty days later he emerged from the wilderness "in the power of the

Spirit" (v. 14). As a result, Jesus "committed no sin" (1 Peter 2:22). Likewise, the Spirit helps us today to overcome temptation and sin in our own lives.

The Spirit once helped me when I was frustrated with one of my children. Our city was covered with snow, so my family and I decided we would go sledding. We all pulled on our snow pants, mittens, and winter jackets, and piled into our minivan to drive across town. When we arrived at the biggest hill in our prairie city, I parked the van at the top. And as we were climbing out with our sleds, one of my daughters said the seven words every parent dreads hearing when their child is all bundled up for winter weather: "I have to go to the bathroom." Of course, there were no bathrooms at the sledding hill or anywhere else within walking distance. "No," I told her. "We just got here . . . And I told you to go to the bathroom before we left the house." She explained that she had gone to the bathroom at home, but that she needed to go again.

I figured we weren't going to have any fun if she was complaining the whole time about needing to go to the bathroom, so I told my wife to stay at the hill with our other children while I drove my daughter to a bathroom. At the time, my wife thought I was being nice, but I grumbled the whole way to the convenience store, and I kept grumbling once we got inside. Then, as I was leaning against the wall outside the bathroom, the Spirit helped me recognize the anger in my heart and convicted me "concerning sin and righteousness" (John 16:8 NASB). And the Spirit didn't just leave me aware of my sin, either. In that moment it was as though the Spirit also gave me a "new heart" (Ezekiel 36:26). I had a choice to live "according to the flesh" or "in accordance with the Spirit" (Romans 8:5), and the Spirit helped me respond to my daughter with patience and gentleness. Our drive back to the sledding hill was a lot more pleasant.

On this occasion the "fruit of the Spirit" became evident in my life. We can choose to give in to temptation and engage in "sexual immorality . . . hatred, discord, jealousy, fits of rage, selfish ambition . . . envy, drunkenness . . . and the like" (Galatians 5:19–21). But the Spirit works to instill "love, joy, peace, patience, kindness, goodness, faithfulness, gentleness, and self-control" (vv. 22–23 NLT). When we exhibit self-control and are kind to someone who stabbed us in the back, we are following the lead of the Spirit. When we are patient with our spouse, even though they are driving us crazy, we show signs of being Spirit-filled. And when we are gentle with those who sin against us, we exhibit the fruit of the Spirit and holiness in our character.

Whenever I talk about character, holiness, and avoiding sin, some people automatically get concerned that I'm being legalistic. Legalism usually refers to rules people, rather than God, set in order to gain God's approval, as though we are saved by our actions rather than grace. While God certainly does have ethical expectations for us, legalism is problematic because it promotes slavery to law rather than freedom from sin. Another problem with legalism is that rules don't change us—the Spirit does. When we are shaped by the Spirit, we don't do what is right only because those who live according to their sinful nature "will not inherit the kingdom of God" (Galatians 5:21). Instead, as the Spirit is poured out upon us like water to cleanse our hearts, the Spirit moves us from having a sense of duty to do what is right, to having delight in obeying God (Psalm 119). Overall, when we exhibit holiness, or the character of Christ, and avoid sin, we are the kind of person that the Bible calls spiritual (Galatians 6:1 NASB).

Proclaiming the Gospel

The Spirit not only enabled Jesus to remain sinless, but the Spirit also empowered Jesus for his ministry. Like the prophets of the Old Testament, who "spoke from God as they were carried along by the Holy Spirit" (2 Peter 1:21), Jesus said he received the Spirit "to proclaim" good news (Luke 4:18). Jesus told the disciples, "You will receive power when the Holy Spirit comes on you; and you will be my witnesses" (Acts 1:8). As a result, the book of Acts records numerous instances when believers "were all filled with the Holy Spirit and spoke the word of God boldly" (Acts 4:31). Another aspect of spirituality, then, is that we are inspired, led, and empowered by the Spirit to share the good news about Jesus Christ by ministering to our family and neighbors, to those in our workplaces, and to others around us.

When I was a teenager, my aunt owned a little white Geo Metro. I lived with her for a couple of summers so I could work in the city, and I occasionally borrowed her car. I could drive her car, and I could get it around, but it was difficult to get her car to go where I wanted it to go because it had manual steering. I especially had to yank on the steering wheel when I was trying to park. By contrast, I now own a long, green minivan that is two or three times as big as that little Geo Metro. But I can get it around easily because it has power in a way the Geo Metro didn't. In fact, I could probably park my minivan using my pinky finger. I don't have to struggle with the steering wheel because I've got power steering. Likewise, the Holy Spirit empowers us to be more effective in our ministry. By contrast, trying to do ministry without the empowerment of the Holy Spirit is like trying to drive a car without power steering.

Miracles

In addition to ministering by proclaiming the good news, Jesus was empowered by the Spirit to do miracles. He said he was anointed with the Spirit to proclaim "recovery of sight for the blind" (Luke 4:18) and that he drove "out demons by the Spirit of God" (Matthew 12:28 NLT). The Gospels are full of stories about Jesus doing miracles, from raising the dead to multiplying food. When Jesus told his disciples they would be "clothed with power from on high" when they received the Holy Spirit (Luke 24:49), this also included their ability to do miracles like Jesus. As a result, after Pentecost, "everyone was filled with awe, and many wonders and miraculous signs were done by the apostles" (Acts 2:43). This empowerment from the Spirit wasn't only for the apostles, though. We find others doing miracles, too, like Stephen, who was "a man full of God's grace and power" and who "performed amazing miracles and signs among the people" (Acts 6:8 NLT).

The Spirit still empowers Christians to do miracles today. We don't receive this ability so we can *look* spiritual. Rather, this is another way the Spirit empowers us to witness (Acts 1:8). In the same way "many people saw the signs [Jesus] was performing and believed in his name" (John 2:23), as Christians perform miracles "through the power of the Spirit of God," the miracles are "signs" pointing people to the truth of the gospel message (Romans 15:19). Therefore, in the first century, when "the apostles performed many signs and wonders among the people . . . , more and more men and women believed in the Lord" (Acts 5:12, 14).

One pastor I know recalls the Spirit doing miracles as he preached the gospel in a rural French community. The church he planted there worshipped in a modest twenty-by-sixty-foot storefront that didn't even have a bathroom. One evening a short, stocky, forty-year-old farmer named Marcel arrived at their church with a lump on his right hand. He walked to the middle of the room and sat on one of the old wooden theater seats the church used as pews. At the end of the service, the pastor stood in front of the congregation and prayed for anyone who needed healing. Still sitting in his seat, Marcel looked down at his hand, and his jaw dropped—the lump was gone. The next time he and the pastor were together, Marcel reported what had happened. Although Marcel had only attended the church a few times in the past, after he was healed, he started inviting other families to the church, and he started hosting Bible studies in his home. God continued to use the pastor to perform miracles in his church as a means of confirming the truth he was preaching. As a result, after a few months the congregation outgrew the location where they were meeting, and they found a larger space to rent for their services.

While some people find the idea of the Spirit empowering them to perform miracles exciting, others find this a little depressing because they don't see it present in their own lives. On one hand, I think we can relieve ourselves of the pressure of expecting to do miracles frequently, given that only some people have the gifts of miracles and healing (1 Corinthians 12:29–30). On the other hand, even though not everyone has the same gifts, this doesn't mean the Spirit can't use us in these areas. As I indicated in a previous chapter, not everyone has the gift of encouragement, but the Spirit can use anyone to encourage others. Likewise, the Spirit can work through anyone to heal another person. But if we never pray for people to be healed, we have no reason to expect that the Spirit will use us to see people healed.

Justice and Care

Jesus was empowered by the Spirit for everything he did in his ministry, and this included his concern for justice and caring for the oppressed. The Old Testament prophets expected that "the Spirit of the LORD" would "rest" on the Messiah, that the Messiah would act with righteousness and justice as he gave "decisions for the poor of the earth" (Isaiah 11:1–4) and that he would "comfort all who mourn" (Isaiah 61:1–2). As the fulfillment of these prophecies, Jesus was anointed with the Spirit to minister "to the poor" and "to set the oppressed free" (Luke 4:18). As a result, Jesus is known for reaching out to the Samaritans (a group despised by Jewish people in the first century), the poor, those the religious people condemned as "sinners," and others who were oppressed. Following the Spirit-inspired example of Christ, when the first Christians were "filled with the Holy Spirit, . . . God's grace was so powerfully at work in them all that there were no needy persons among them" (Acts 4:31,

33–34). Likewise, the Spirit causes Christians today to be concerned about social justice issues. By the empowerment of the Spirit, many advocate for and minister to oppressed people in our own contexts, whether they are racially, physically, or even religiously oppressed.

A number of years ago, I read a letter to the editor in a Pentecostal magazine. The author declared that he wanted the magazine to publish more "research on the activity of the Holy Spirit." It seemed that this person had a limited view of the ways the Spirit works, though, because he clarified that he wanted to read more stories "of God's miraculous power at work" in the church. I was curious what this person might have been reacting to, so I leafed through the previous issue of the magazine and found a story about a church that had purchased a strip club across the road and turned it into a community center to reach out to the oppressed in their community. I thought, *That right there* is *the activity of the Holy Spirit.* This church exhibited signs of spirituality as they cared for the oppressed around them, just like Jesus, who is the epitome of spirituality.

Devotion

Another sign of being Spirit-filled is an increasing sense of devotion as we express our faith in God. Just as Jesus prayed, "Abba, Father" (Mark 14:36), when we receive the Spirit we become children of God and the Spirit enables us, too, to cry "Abba, Father" (Romans 8:15). We "pray in the Spirit on all occasions with all kinds of prayers and requests" (Ephesians 6:18), and when we come to the point where we do not even know what to pray, "the Spirit Himself intercedes for us with groanings too deep for words" (Romans 8:26 NASB).

Along with prayer, after the first Christians received the Spirit at Pentecost, "they devoted themselves to the apostles' teaching and to the fellowship, [and] to the breaking of bread" (Acts 2:42). Similarly, when I was a teenager and began to experience more of the work of the Spirit in my life, my growing sense of passion for and devotion to God was probably the most noticeable change in my life. Like the first Christians whose devotion led them to daily "meet together in the temple courts" (v. 46), I was eager to regularly gather at church with other Christians to worship God. Not only that, but I also went to as many church camps as I could—I volunteered at kids camp as a counsellor, and I attended youth and family camp. And at the end of a camp service, you could pretty much always find me in prayer at the altar. Even when I wasn't in a church service, I was devoted to encountering God in Scripture, and my parents would often find me asleep in my bed with my reading lamp still on because I fell asleep reading the Bible, not because it was boring, but because it was getting late. And the Spirit not only guided me "into all the truth" (John 16:13), but the Spirit drove me there. Jesus said the Spirit "will glorify" him (John 16:14), and that is exactly what happened as my desire for and devotion to God grew and I grew in my spirituality.

Christian Community

Being Spirit-filled concerns more than just personal experiences of the Holy Spirit, for the Spirit leads us to engage in Christian community. The Spirit who compels us to preach and serve in the world at large also draws us together. When we became believers, "we were all baptized by one Spirit so as to form one body" (1 Corinthians 12:13). And as I indicated in the previous chapter, we receive spiritual gifts "so that the church may be built up" (1 Corinthians 14:26).

The Spirit we received encourages us to remain in community with other Christians. We were never meant to live out our faith in isolation. And taking in the occasional Christian TV show or podcast is not sufficient. After Jesus poured out the Spirit on the day of Pentecost, the newly Spirit-filled Christians "continued to meet together in the temple courts." And "they broke bread in their homes and ate together with glad and sincere hearts" (Acts 2:46).

We see aspects of the value of Christian community in the last chapter of Romans. Here Paul commended Phoebe who, he said, "has been *helpful to many*, and especially to me" (Romans 16:2 NLT). And he sent "greetings to Priscilla and Aquila," his "*co-workers in the ministry* of Christ Jesus" (v. 3). They had "once risked their lives for" him (v. 4), Paul said, and they hosted church meetings in their home (v. 5). Paul also reminded the Romans of Mary, "who worked very hard for" their benefit (v. 6), and he sent his greetings to Andronicus and Junia, who had been in prison with Paul (v. 7). Among others Paul also mentioned Ampliatus, his "*dear friend* in the Lord" (v. 8), and Rufus's mother, who had "*been a mother* to" Paul (v. 13). In my own life, I have felt the love of Christian community as the Spirit has led people in my church to "rejoice with those who rejoice"— for example, after the birth of a child—and to "mourn with those who mourn"—like after a loved one has passed away (Romans 12:15). All I have described in this paragraph is part of what it means to experience the "fellowship of the Holy Spirit" (2 Corinthians 13:14).

Although the "family of God" (the church) may have squabbles, like any family, we need to "make every effort to keep the unity of the Spirit through the bond of peace" (Ephesians 4:3). This means we love one another as we serve one another, forgive one another, bear with one another, encourage one another, care for one another, and honor one another. By contrast, if we provoke and envy one another and cause disunity in the church, we are not being led by the Spirit. We need to protect the church because the church continues to be a people who are "being built together to become a dwelling in which God lives by his Spirit"

(Ephesians 2:22). As a result, the Bible refers to the church (the people, not buildings) as "God's temple," and we are warned that "if anyone destroys God's temple, God will destroy that person" (1 Corinthians 3:17). We show signs of spirituality, then, as we remain in community with other Christians and contribute to the unity of the church.

Spiritual ≠ Victory

Some people incorrectly think people who are really Spirit-filled will always experience victory. This belief is a cousin to the idea that if you have enough faith you will always experience health and wealth. Just as faith doesn't guarantee a life free of disappointments and hardships, the Spirit-filled life is not a life free of disappointments and hardships. Jesus is the epitome of spirituality, but he never became an earthly king. Instead, "through the eternal Spirit [he] offered himself unblemished to God" so his death might give us life (Hebrews 9:14). In the Bible, "the one who is victorious" (Revelation 2:11) may suffer and face poverty (v. 9). Their victory is that they resist their culture's anti-Christian values and are "faithful, even to the point of death" (v. 10). And their "victor's crown" is eternal life, not achieving success in the eyes of the world around them (vv. 10–11).

The Spirit's empowerment may at times lead to great successes, but it doesn't guarantee them. Barnabas, for example, "was a good man, full of the Holy Spirit and faith" and through his ministry "a great number of people were brought to the Lord" (Acts 11:22–24). By contrast, Stephen, who was also "a man full of faith and of the Holy Spirit" (Acts 6:5 and 7:55), was stoned to death when he preached the gospel (7:58). Similarly, Peter and Paul both had their lives threatened and were imprisoned on account of Christ, but they continued to preach the gospel because they had power and boldness from the Holy Spirit. Today the Spirit continues to inspire people to stay committed to Christ in the face of adversity, even to the point of martyrdom.

Aside from the fact that those we minister to can "resist the Holy Spirit" (Acts 7:51) and, therefore, our Spirit-empowered ministry is not always well-received, we live in a fallen creation that is yet to "be liberated from its bondage to decay" (Romans 8:21). As a consequence, even though we "have the firstfruits of the Spirit," we "groan inwardly as we wait eagerly for our adoption to sonship, the redemption of our bodies" (v. 23). However, as we long with hope, God does not abandon us, for "the Spirit helps us in our weakness" (v. 26). As James Dunn observed, the Spirit is not only present "in the heights of spiritual rapture," but also "in the depths of human inability to cope."[2] This means that if we find ourselves outside of some experiences of victory, this is not necessarily a sign of a lack of spirituality—in fact, at those times the Spirit might be particularly active in our lives.

Spiritual ≠ Perfect

The presence of the Spirit in our lives also doesn't mean that we will be perfect and never make mistakes. Jesus is the only person who has ever been sinless. And so, the Spirit continues to work through imperfect people. In the Old Testament, I think of Gideon, who served as one of Israel's Judges: "The Spirit of the LORD came on Gideon" and he rallied the Israelites to stand together in solidarity against the Midianites and Amalekites who had been oppressing them (Judges 6:34). In spite of this, Gideon was fearful and doubted God's promise to save Israel (v. 27). So Gideon twice asked God to perform a miraculous sign to confirm God's promise (vv. 36–40). And Samson, another one of Israel's judges, had faults that are well known. Although the Spirit came powerfully upon him on numerous occasions (Judges 13:25; 14:6, 19; 15:14), he dishonored his parents (14:2–6), he allowed Delilah to manipulate him (14:16; 16:15), and he was motivated by revenge (15:3, 11). To top it all off, he even slept with a prostitute (16:1). Even though the Spirit of God was at work in both Gideon and Samson, these men didn't become exemplary or even ideal figures.[3] Instead, like all of us, they remained imperfect, finite, mortal human beings. And yet, somehow, the New Testament affirms *both* Gideon and Samson as examples of faith (Hebrews 11:32).

Even as we move from the Old Testament to the New Testament, we find that believers still struggle between living "according the Spirit" and living "according to the flesh" (or "sinful nature") (Romans 8:5–6). We see, for example, how Peter's experience of the Spirit at Pentecost transformed him from someone who had denied three times that he knew Jesus to someone who stood in front of a crowd to preach the gospel (Acts 2:14–41). And yet Paul had to correct Peter (a Jew) because he refused to eat with Gentiles (non-Jews) (Galatians 2:11–14).

When we look at these stories, we are reminded that when the Spirit works in and through us, it is a mark of God's grace, not of our moral superiority. At times I am tempted to think that the Spirit can't or won't use me because of my imperfections. I confess that I also sometimes think this way about others. But when I remember the imperfect characters the Spirit used in the Bible, I am reminded that God's "power is made perfect in weakness" (2 Corinthians 12:9).

Increasing Spirituality

The previous section implies that we can increasingly live a more spiritual or Spirit-filled life. On one hand, because we are born again by the Spirit (John 3:3, 8), we can correctly say that every Christian is a "spiritual person" (1 Corinthians 2:15 ESV). On the other hand, even though Paul was writing to believers, he said to the Corinthians, "I could not address you as spiritual people, but as people of the flesh, as infants in Christ" (1 Corinthians 3:1–2). Spiritual growth, then, is possible inasmuch as the presence of the Spirit can intensify in our lives as we grow as Christians.[4] For example, while the disciples were able to engage in ministry before Pentecost and even saw people healed (Luke 9:1), at Pentecost they received more power from the Spirit (Acts 1:8) and became even more effective in their ministry. And the Spirit can always shape our character to be more like Christ. Indeed, we increase our spirituality as, by the Spirit, we "are being transformed into his image" (2 Corinthians 3:18). As this happens, we become more spiritual.

So, how do we become more spiritual? By the Spirit working in our lives. To some extent, then, being Spirit-filled is not something we can control, at least insofar as we can't make the Spirit do anything. At the same time, the Spirit is like the wind blowing into a ship's sail—when the Spirit blows in our lives, we can adjust our sails to harness the wind's power. In other words, we can cooperate with and submit to the work of the Spirit. The fruit of the Spirit illustrates this well. On one hand, fruit doesn't grow by itself—the Spirit is the one who instills in us "love, joy, peace, patience, kindness, goodness, faithfulness, gentleness and self-control" (Galatians 5:22–23 NLT). On the other hand, we need to be "led by the Spirit" (v. 18 NIV) to see the fruit grow. This is true of all areas of spirituality. Like dancers, where the Spirit leads we must follow as we "keep in step with the Spirit" (v. 25). Sometimes we seem to initiate the dance by engaging in spiritual disciplines, such as prayer, fasting, and worship. At other times the Spirit invites us to join the dance by prompting us to respond to something God is telling us to do or not do. At times we dance with more elegance than other times; and, as a result, we all have some areas where we can still aim to increase our spirituality.

What Does It Mean to Be Spirit-filled?

Being Spirit-filled, or being spiritual, comes about as we submit to the work of the Spirit in our lives. Although the Spirit inspires worship, our spirituality isn't dependent on how we worship—whether we prefer to be quiet and still, or loud and animated. As we think back to all I have said in this book, we see that spirituality can include having intense, even physically intense, responses to the Spirit. It can include the Spirit guiding us and speaking to us in various ways. It might involve speaking in tongues. And it might also include having great faith and witnessing people being healed. Being Spirit-filled might express itself in serving others through gifts the Spirit gives us. In this chapter, we've seen that spirituality can include unusual experiences, like dreams and visions. It also involves the Spirit shaping our character to be like Jesus'. And our spirituality includes being empowered by the Spirit to minister by proclaiming the gospel with our words, through miracles, and by caring for the oppressed. Finally, a rise in spirituality increases our devotion to both God and other Christians in the church community.

Some aspects of the Spirit-filled life are less visible than others. Therefore, we shouldn't assume that if a person's spirituality is particularly noticeable, that person is necessarily more spiritual than others. We can experience the Spirit in a variety of ways and, therefore, express our spirituality in different ways.

The experience of the Spirit is ultimately an experience of the love of God, for "God's love has been poured out into our hearts through the Holy Spirit, who has been given to us" (Romans 5:5). As a result, being Spirit-filled ultimately means we become like Jesus by showing love toward God and others. Through this, we fulfill the greatest commandments and God's very purpose for our lives. It does not matter if you *act* in a way that *appears* spiritual: "The only thing that counts is faith expressing itself through love" (Galatians 5:6).

Father, forgive us if we have had poor attitudes toward others we thought were not as spiritual as us, even if only because we had a limited view of how the Spirit works. Please help us realize where we have resisted the Holy Spirit. Make us open to all the ways you want to work in us by the Spirit and help us keep in step with the Spirit.

May the presence and work of the Spirit increase within us each day.

Questions for Reflection or Discussion

1. Before reading this chapter, how would you have defined what it means for a Christian to be "spiritual" or "Spirit-filled"? In what ways has your thinking developed?
2. What keeps some people from being open to the work of the Spirit in their lives?
3. Have you ever thought other people were less spiritual than you because they responded to the Spirit in different ways than you do?
4. How do you see the Spirit at work in your own life? Are there any areas where you still need to respond in obedience to the Spirit?
5. Who can you encourage this week by helping them see a way the Spirit is working through them?

I pray that out of his glorious riches he may strengthen you with power through his Spirit in your inner being, so that Christ may dwell in your hearts through faith. And I pray that you, being rooted and established in love, may have power, together with all the Lord's holy people, to grasp how wide and long and high and deep is the love of Christ, and to know this love that surpasses knowledge—that you may be filled to the measure of all the fullness of God. Now to him who is able to do immeasurably more than all we ask or imagine, according to his power that is at work within us, to him be glory in the church and in Christ Jesus through-out all generations, for ever and ever! Amen.

(EPHESIANS 3:16–21)

ACKNOWLEDGMENTS

I pray that this book has encouraged you to fully embrace life in the Spirit. I thank God for the many people who have helped me make this book better for you than it otherwise might have been. Many of these people know more about experiencing the Spirit than I do. To begin, numerous friends, including many pastors, read through one or two chapters and offered helpful suggestions. And so I sincerely thank Carmen Kampman, Gwen Hacking, Alan Duncalfe, Mike Hatheway, Brian Webb, Tammy Junghans, Trudy Unger, Dan Murphy, Kevin Johnson, Brandon Malo, John-Mark Morley, Stephen Shew, Scott Eastveld, Ben Wright, Brad Thomas, Derek Kennedy, Vern Kratz, Randy Raycroft, and my father, Dennis Gabriel.

Though I wrote this book for a general audience of lay people, pastors, and students, I also wanted to ensure a level of academic rigor, and so I am also grateful for numerous friends who serve as professors of the Bible or theology and who were willing to take the time to give me feedback on a chapter. This includes Marty Mittelstadt, Brad Noel, Josh Samuel, Jeromey Martini, Randy Holm, David Courey, Peter Neumann, and Chris Thomas. I would also like to thank my office neighbor, Leanne Bellamy, who used her expertise in all things English to help me strengthen my writing, and my teaching assistant, Alyssa Andrews, whose help allowed me the time to complete this book and who offered a number of suggestions for the book itself.

Sometimes I was optimistic, at other times pessimistic, about the prospects of publishing this book. And so, I am also grateful for the prayers and encouragement of the students and staff at Horizon College and Seminary, where I serve as a professor. This includes especially Jeromey Martini, Ron Kadyschuk, and Carmen Kampman. Outside of my college community, I would also like to thank Brian Stiller and David Wells, who cheered me on as I neared the end of this book project.

I'm particularly thankful for a loving and supportive family. My three girls, Rayelle, Mylah, and Adelyn, keep the joy quotient high in my life. And I would especially like to thank my wife, Krista, who offered many constructive suggestions for my book. More importantly, I'm thankful that she continues to love me despite the fact that I'm a theologian. While my academic writing hasn't often been attractive to her, I am encouraged to know that she feels this book is actually worth reading—and she did read the whole thing!

NOTES

Chapter 2: Shake and Bake

1. "Pentecost Has Come," *The Apostolic Faith* 1, no. 1 (September 1906): 1.
2. John McAlister, "Reports from Western Canada," *The Pentecostal Testimony* 1 (December 1920): 2.
3. Jonathan Edwards, "The Distinguishing Marks of the Work of the Spirit of God," in *Jonathan Edwards on Revival* (Edinburgh: The Banner of Truth Trust, 1984), 64.
4. John Wesley, *The Works of John Wesley*, 3rd ed., vol. 1 (Grand Rapids: Baker, 1979), 210.
5. ———, *The Works of John Wesley*, 196 (original emphasis).
6. ———, *The Works of John Wesley*, 196.
7. Quoted in Vinson Synan, *The Holiness–Pentecostal Tradition: Charismatic Movements in the Twentieth Century*, 2nd ed. (Grand Rapids: Eerdmans, 1997), 13.

8. Jack Deere, *Surprised by the Power of the Spirit: A Former Dallas Seminary Professor Discovers That God Speaks and Heals Today* (Grand Rapids: Zondervan, 1993), 92.

9. Cited in Douglas Jacobsen, *Thinking in the Spirit: Theologies of the Early Pentecostal Movement* (Bloomington, IN: Indiana University Press, 2003), 147–48.

10. Marvin Gorman, "Slain in the Spirit," in *Conference on the Holy Spirit Digest*, vol. 2, ed. Gwen Jones (Springfield, MO: Gospel Publishing House, 1983), 305.

11. Laurence J. Barber, "How I Was Blessed," *Christianity Today* (September 11, 1995): 26.

Chapter 3: Knock, Knock. Who's There?

1. Gordon T. Smith, "Learning to Listen: The Relationship View," in *How Then Should We Choose? Three Views of God's Will and Decision Making*, ed. Douglas S. Huffman (Grand Rapids: Kregel, 2009), 181.

2. Brad Jersak, *Can You Hear Me? Tuning in to the God Who Speaks* (Abbotsford, BC: Fresh Wind Press, 2003), 19.

3. The following questions are based on a "Listening Survey" in Jersak, *Can You Hear Me?*, 27–36.

4. Dan Bremnes, "In His Hands," *Where the Light Is*, Sparrow Records, 2015.

5. Jason Gray, "Sparrows," *Where the Light Gets In*, Centricity Music, 2016.

6. Jack Deere, *Surprised by the Power of the Spirit*, 215.

7. Bill Hybels, *The Power of a Whisper: Hearing God, Having the Guts to Respond* (Grand Rapids: Zondervan, 2010), 105–6.

Chapter 4: Crazy Talk

1. Acts 2:8 is the only place in Acts that indicates that speaking in tongues was understood by people who were listening. And in that instance, it was not because anyone was interpreting the tongues being spoken.
2. Frank Macchia, *Baptized in the Spirit: A Global Pentecostal Theology* (Grand Rapids: Zondervan, 2006), 13.
3. Randall Holm, "Tongues as a Blush in the Presence of God," *Journal of Pentecostal Theology* 20 (2011): 130.
4. Ellen Hebden, "How Pentecost Came to Toronto," *The Promise* 1 (May 1907): 1–2.

Chapter 5: Living Large

1. Quoted by Kate Bowler, *Blessed: A History of the American Prosperity Gospel* (Oxford: Oxford University Press, 2013), 249.
2. Kenneth Copeland, *The Laws of Prosperity* (Fort Worth, TX: Kenneth Copeland Publications, 1974), 17, emphasis added.
3. Joseph Prince, *Destined to Reign: The Secret to Effortless Success, Wholeness and Victorious Living* (Tulsa, OK: Harrison House, 2007), 1, emphasis added.
4. Regarding (primarily) Americans, see Lewis Brogdon, *The New Pentecostal Message? An Introduction to the Prosperity Movement* (Eugene, OR: Cascade, 2015), 6–24; and Bowler, *Blessed*, 239, 252–54. Canadian prosperity preachers do not typically have the same fame as their American counterparts. Regarding Canadians, see Catherine Bowler, "From Far and Wide: The Canadian Faith Movement," *Church and Faith Trends* 3, no. 1

(February 2010): 2 and 5, available at http://files.efc-canada
.net/min/rc/cft/V03I01/Canadian_Faith_Movement.pdf
(accessed June 11, 2014).

5. Kenneth E. Hagin, *Exceedingly Growing Faith* (Tulsa, OK:
   Kenneth Hagin Ministries, 1973), 40.
6. Gordon D. Fee, *The Disease of the Health and Wealth
   Gospels* (Vancouver, BC: Regent College, 1985), 26.
7. Larry D. Hart, *Truth Aflame: Theology for the Church in
   Renewal*, rev. ed. (Grand Rapids: Zondervan, 2005), 196,
   original emphasis.
8. Copeland, *Laws of Prosperity*, 19.
9. Hagin, *Exceedingly Growing Faith*, 102.
10. Hagin, *Exceedingly Growing Faith*, 102.
11. Oral Roberts, *Expect a New Miracle Every Day* (Tulsa,
    OK: Oral Roberts Evangelistic Association, 1963), 22–23.
12. Peter H. Davids, *A Theology of James, Peter, and Jude*,
    Biblical Theology of the New Testament Series (Grand
    Rapids: Zondervan, 2014), 50.
13. Frederick K. C. Price, *Faith, Foolishness, or Presumption?*
    (Tulsa, OK: Harrison House, 1979), 111 and 123.
14. R. Alan Cole, *The Gospel According to St. Mark:
    An Introduction and Commentary*, Tyndale New
    Testament Commentaries (Grand Rapids: Eerdmans,
    1961), 181.
15. R. T. France, *The Gospel of Matthew*, The New
    International Commentary on the New Testament (Grand
    Rapids: Eerdmans, 2007), 589–91.
16. Ronald A. N. Kydd, *Healing Through the Centuries:
    Models for Understanding* (Peabody, MA: Hendrickson,
    1998).

Chapter 6: Measuring Up?

1. Yves Congar, *I Believe in the Holy Spirit*, vol. 2 of *He Is Lord and Giver of Life,* trans. David Smith (New York: Crossroad, 1983), 165, 173.

2. To be fair, Paul did use the singular form "spiritual gift" in one place—Romans 1:11. However, there the term was not used in the context of or with the meaning of what most people think of with respect to "spiritual gifts."

3. Stanley M. Burgess, "Evidence of the Spirit: The Ancient and Eastern Churches," and "Evidence of the Spirit: The Medieval and Modern Western Churches," in *Initial Evidence: Historical and Biblical Perspectives on the Pentecostal Doctrine of Spirit Baptism*, ed. Gary B. McGee (Peabody, MA: Hendrickson, 1991), 3–40.

4. Anthony C. Thiselton, *The First Epistle to the Corinthians*, The New International Greek Testament Commentary (Grand Rapids: Eerdmans, 2013), 941.

5. From the first and second century, see *Didache* in *The Apostolic Fathers*, vol. 1, ed. and trans. Bart D. Ehrman, The Loeb Classical Library, vol. 24 (Cambridge, MA: Harvard University Press, 2003), chapters 11–13 and 435–39; and *Shepherd of Hermas* in *The Apostolic Fathers*, vol. 2, ed. and trans. Bart D. Ehrman, The Loeb Classical Library, vol. 25 (Cambridge, MA: Harvard University Press, 2003), Commandment 11 (43.7–8, 12) and 287–89.

6. Gordon Fee, *God's Empowering Presence: The Holy Spirit in the Letters of Paul* (Peabody, MA: Hendrickson, 1994), 195–97 and 214–20.

7. For example, https://spiritualgiftstest.com /spiritual-gifts-test-adult-version/.

8. Sydney Page, "The Assumptions Behind Spiritual Gifts Inventories," *Didaskalia* 22 (Fall 2011): 39–59.

9. Clark H. Pinnock, "Church in the Power of the Holy Spirit: The Promise of Pentecostal Ecclesiology," *Journal of Pentecostal Theology* 14, no. 2 (2006): 147–65.

Chapter 7: What Does It Mean to Be Spirit-Filled?

1. Gordon D. Fee, *God's Empowering Presence*, 29.

2. James D. G. Dunn, *Word Biblical Commentary: Romans 1–8*, vol. 38A (Dallas, TX: Word, 1988), 479.

3. Michael Welker, *God the Spirit*, trans. John F. Hoffmeyer (Minneapolis, MN: Fortress, 1994), 59–60.

4. Andrew K. Gabriel, "The Intensity of the Spirit in a Spirit-Filled World: Spirit Baptism, Subsequence, and the Spirit of Creation," *Pneuma: The Journal of the Society for Pentecostal Studies* 34, no. 3 (2012): 365–82.

ABOUT THE AUTHOR

Dr. Andrew K. Gabriel is an ordained minister who serves as associate professor of theology and vice president of academics at Horizon College and Seminary. He is a member of the Theological Study Commission of the Pentecostal Assemblies of Canada and the author of three books, including *The Lord Is the Spirit*. Andrew and his family live in Saskatoon, Saskatchewan, Canada.

Read more from Andrew at www.andrewkgabriel.com.